# 新双双中文教材 8
New Chinese Language and Culture Course

## 中国古代故事 *Ancient Chinese Stories*

王双双　编著

北京大学出版社　PEKING UNIVERSITY PRESS

NanHai
BRIDGING EAST & WEST

图书在版编目（CIP）数据

中国古代故事/ 王双双编著. —2版. —北京：北京大学出版社，2018.9（2022.1重印）
（新双双中文教材）
ISBN 978-7-301-29225-9

Ⅰ.①中…　Ⅱ.①王…　Ⅲ.①汉语—对外汉语教学—教材　②历史故事—作品集—中国
Ⅳ.①H195.4

中国版本图书馆CIP数据核字（2018）第026779号

| | |
|---|---|
| 书　　　名 | 中国古代故事（第二版）<br>ZHONGGUO GUDAI GUSHI（DI-ER BAN） |
| 著作责任者 | 王双双　编著 |
| 英文翻译 | [德] Nanny Kim（金兰中） |
| 责任编辑 | 邓晓霞 |
| 标准书号 | ISBN 978-7-301-29225-9 |
| 出版发行 | 北京大学出版社 |
| 地　　　址 | 北京市海淀区成府路205号　100871 |
| 网　　　址 | http://www.pup.cn　　新浪微博：@北京大学出版社 |
| 电子信箱 | zpup@pup.cn |
| 电　　　话 | 邮购部 010-62752015　发行部 010-62750672　编辑部 010-62767349 |
| 印　刷　者 | 三河市博文印刷有限公司 |
| 经　销　者 | 新华书店 |
| | 889毫米×1194毫米　16开本　10.5印张　94千字<br>2006年7月第1版<br>2018年9月第2版　2022年3月第3次印刷 |
| 定　　　价 | 80.00元（含课本、练习本） |

未经许可，不得以任何方式复制或抄袭本书之部分或全部内容。
**版权所有，侵权必究**
举报电话：010-62752024　电子信箱：fd@pup.pku.edu.cn
图书如有印装质量问题，请与出版部联系，电话：010-62756370

# 第二版序

能够与北京大学出版社合作出版"双双中文教材"的第二版，让这套优秀的对外汉语教材泽被更多的学生，加州中文教学研究中心备感荣幸。

这是一套洋溢着浓浓爱意的教材。作者的女儿在美国出生，到了识字年龄，作者教她学习过市面上流行的多套中文教材，但都强烈地感觉到这些教材"水土不服"。一解女儿学习中文的燃眉之急，是作者编写这套教材的初衷和原动力。为了让没有中文环境的孩子能够喜欢学习中文，作者字斟句酌地编写课文；为了赋予孩子审美享受、引起他们的共鸣，作者特邀善画儿童创作了一幅幅稚气可爱的插图；为了加深孩子们对内容的理解，激发孩子们的学习热情，作者精心设计了充满创造性的互动活动。

这是一套承载着文化传承使命感的教材。语言不仅仅是文化的载体，更是文化重要的有机组成部分。学习一门外语的深层障碍往往根植于目标语言与母语间的文化差异。这种差异对于学习中文的西方学生尤为突出。这套教材的使用对象正处在好奇心和好胜心最强的年龄阶段，作者抓住了这一特点，变阻力为动力，一改过去削学生认知能力和智力水平之"足"以适词汇和语言知识之"履"的通病。教材在高年级部分，一个学期一个文化主题，以对博大精深的中国文化的探索激发学生的学习兴趣，使学生在学习语言的同时了解璀璨的中国文化。

"双双中文教材"自2005年面世以来，受到了老师、学生和家长的广泛欢迎。很多觉得中文学习枯燥无味而放弃的学生，因这套教材发现了学习中文的乐趣，又重新回到了中文课堂。本次修订，作者不仅吸纳了老师们对于初版的反馈意见和自己实际使用过程中的心得，还参考了近年对外汉语教学理论及实践方面的成果。语言学习部分由原来的九册改为五册，一学年学习一册，文化学习部分保持一个专题一册。相信修订后的"新双双中文教材"会更方便、实用，让更多学生受益。

张晓江
美国加州中文教学研究中心秘书长

# 第一版前言

"双双中文教材"是一套专门为海外青少年编写的中文课本，是我在美国八年的中文教学实践基础上编写成的。在介绍这套教材之前，请读一首小诗：

> 一双神奇的手，
> 推开一扇窗。
> 一条神奇的路，
> 通向灿烂的中华文化。

鲍凯文　鲍维江

鲍维江和鲍凯文姐弟俩是美国生美国长的孩子，也是我的学生。1998年冬，他们送给我的新年贺卡上的小诗，深深地打动了我的心。我把这首诗看成我文化教学的"回声"。我要传达给海外每位中文老师：我教给他们（学生）中国文化，他们思考了、接受了、回应了。这条路走通了！

语言是一种交流的工具，更是一种文化和一种生活方式，所以学习中文也就离不开中华文化的学习。汉字是一种古老的象形文字，她从远古走来，带有大量的文化信息，但学起来并不容易。使学生增强兴趣、减小难度，走出苦学汉字的怪圈，走进领悟中华文化的花园，是我编写这套教材的初衷。

学生不论大小，天生都有求知的欲望，都有欣赏文化美的追求。中华文化本身是魅力十足的。把这宏大而玄妙的文化，深入浅出地，有声有色地介绍出来，让这迷人的文化如涓涓细流，一点一滴地渗入学生们的心田，使学生们逐步体味中国文化，是我编写这套教材的目的。

为此我将汉字的学习放入文化介绍的流程之中同步进行，让同学们在学中国地理的同时，学习汉字；在学中国历史的同时，学习汉字；在学中国哲学的同时，学习汉字；在学中国科普文选的同时，学习汉字……

这样的一种中文学习，知识性强，趣味性强；老师易教，学生易学。当学生们合上书本时，他们的眼前是中国的大好河山，是中国五千年的历史和妙不可言的哲学思维，是奔腾的现代中国……

总之，他们了解了中华文化，就会探索这片土地，热爱这片土地，就会与中国结下情缘。

最后我要衷心地感谢所有热情支持和帮助我编写教材的老师、家长、学生、朋友和家人。特别是老同学唐玲教授、何茜老师和我女儿Uta Guo年复一年的鼎力相助。可以说这套教材是大家努力的结果。

王双双

# 课程设置（建议）

| 序号 | 书名 | 适用年级 |
|---|---|---|
| 1 | 中文课本　第一册 | 幼儿园/一年级 |
| 2 | 中文课本　第二册 | 二年级 |
| 3 | 中文课本　第三册 | 三年级 |
| 4 | 中文课本　第四册 | 四年级 |
| 5 | 中文课本　第五册 | 五年级 |
| 6 | 中国成语故事 | 六年级 |
| 7 | 中国地理常识 | 六年级 |
| 8 | 中国古代故事 | 七年级 |
| 9 | 中国神话传说 | 七年级 |
| 10 | 中国古代科学技术 | 八年级 |
| 11 | 中国民俗与民间艺术 | 八年级 |
| 12 | 中国文学欣赏 | 九年级 |
| 13 | 中国诗歌欣赏 | 九年级 |
| 14 | 中国古代哲学 | 十年级 |
| 15 | 中国历史 | 十年级 |

# 目录

第一课　曹冲称象 …………………………………… 1

第二课　田忌赛马 …………………………………… 11

第三课　李寄杀蛇 …………………………………… 19

第四课　晏子使楚 …………………………………… 28

第五课　西门豹的故事 ……………………………… 36

第六课　张良拜师 …………………………………… 44

第七课　三试华佗 …………………………………… 53

第八课　高山流水 …………………………………… 62

第九课　七步诗 ……………………………………… 71

第十课　完璧归赵 …………………………………… 78

生字表（简）………………………………………… 87

生字表（繁）………………………………………… 88

生词表（简）………………………………………… 89

生词表（繁）………………………………………… 91

附录　"新双双中文教材"写作练习（1—8册）… 93

# 第一课

## 曹冲称象

古时候,有个人叫曹操,他是东汉末期的政治家、军事家和诗人。有一次,人家送他一头大象。曹操非常高兴,带着儿子和官员们一同去看大象。

大象又高又大,身体像一面墙,腿像四根大柱子。这象到底有多重呢?官员们议论着。曹操问官员们:"谁能有办法把这头大象称一称?"有人说:"用一棵大树造一杆大秤来称,或者把大象宰了,切成一块一块的再称。"也有人说:"有了大秤也不成啊,谁有那么大的力气,提得起这杆大秤呢?再说把大象宰了,虽然能称出它的重量,可是以后,就再也没有大象了!"

刘艺 画

曹操听了官员们的话，直摇头，说："难道就没有别的办法了吗？"曹操的儿子曹冲才六岁，他站出来说："我有好办法。"曹操连忙问儿子有什么办法。曹冲说："把大象赶到一条大船上，沿着水面在船舷(xián)上画一道线。再把大象赶上岸，往船上装石头，等船下沉到画线的地方，称一称船上的石头，就知道大象有多重了。"

曹操很高兴，说："这是个好办法。"于是叫人照着曹冲说的办法去做，果然称出了大象的重量。官员们一个个脸都红了，你看看我，我看看你，觉得自己还不如一个六岁的孩子。

第一课

## 生 词

| | | | |
|---|---|---|---|
| chēng 称 | weigh | huòzhě 或者 | or |
| mò qī 末期 | at the end of | zǎi 宰 | slay |
| guān yuán 官员 | officer | qiē 切 | cut |
| zhù 柱 | column | nándào 难道 | used in a rhetorical question for emphasis |
| dào dǐ 到底 | on earth | liánmáng 连忙 | promptly |
| yì lùn 议论 | discuss | gǎn 赶 | drive |
| gǎn 杆 | measure word for balances, etc. | yán zhe 沿着 | along |
| chèng 秤 | balance | | |

## 听 写

称　官员　到底　沿着　议论　切　或者　秤

杆　赶　*末期

注：*号以后的为听写选做题。

## 比一比

主（主人）　　　称（称一称）　　　员 ｛官员
柱（柱子）　　　秤（一杆秤）　　　　　飞行员

中国古代故事

| 秤 | 称 |
|---|---|
| （名）称量工具 | （动）量轻重 |

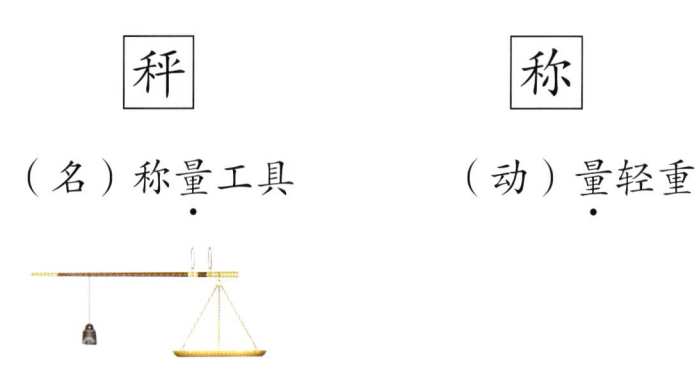

## 同音字

带　代　袋　戴

带 { 带着 / 安全带 }　　代 { 代表 / 古代 }

袋 { 口袋 / 袋鼠 }　　戴 { 戴帽子 / 戴手表 }

## 字词运用

**难道**

① 难道你不知道老鼠怕猫吗？

② 难道你不知道今天有大雨吗？

③ 妹妹都能学会，难道我就学不会吗？

或者

① 我午饭吃包子或者面条儿都行。

② 我打算明天或者后天回北京。

③ 同学们来这里可以打球或者下棋。

沿着

① 我们沿着河边往前走。

② 沿着公路的两边都种上了树。

## 词语解释

议论——大家都说出自己的意见。

不如——比不上。

## 阅读

### 曹冲

曹冲（196—208），是曹操的一个儿子。曹冲从小聪明，也有爱心，曹操很喜爱他。他六岁时，就有办法称出大象的重量。曹冲还常常帮助人。一次曹操的东西被老鼠咬坏了，仆人吓哭了。曹冲看到，就把自己的衣服挖了一些洞，对曹操说是老鼠咬的。曹操感到老鼠太多，谁也没办法，就放过了仆人。不过曹冲十三岁时因病去世了，曹操非常悲痛。

### 我从汉朝来

打开汉语字典，找到"汉"字，你会读到：汉朝、汉字、汉人、汉族、汉语、汉学、汉水……这么多的词语中都有"汉"字，这是怎么回事呢？

西安城上的繁体"汉"字

公元前206年，刘邦建立了汉朝，前后400多年。汉朝，是汉民族的青年时期，生机勃勃，像个年轻人带着对生活的热爱和满脑子的想象力，创造着自己的文化，发展经济，扩大疆土。和西方的罗马帝国一样，东方的中国在汉朝时成为文明先进、统一强盛的国家。汉朝积极与外国交往，开始走向世界。从此，他们的语言叫"汉语"，书写的字叫"汉字"，华夏民族逐渐(zhú jiàn)被称为"汉族"。

汉朝：公元前206年—公元220年。

汉族：中国人数最多的民族。

汉语：汉民族的语言。

汉字：记录(lù)汉语的文字。

## 中国古代故事

> 资料

## 汉朝画像石欣赏

汉画像石十分生动美丽。汉代人画出了一幅幅充满活力和热闹的世界。下面的两图，分别是"飞人"坐在"马身飞鸟"拉的车上，河伯坐在大鱼拉的车上。一个自由浪漫的神仙世界。

朏(fēi)鸟驾鸟顶车

神话故事，驾车的鸟是马身马腿，乘车的人是鸟翅人首，后边的随从也是长翅膀的。

河南南阳王庄汉墓出土画像石　　河伯（河神）出行

## Cao Chong Weighed an Elephant

Long, long ago, Cao Cao was a famous politician, military leader and poet. He lived around the end of the Eastern Han Dynasty. One day, Cao Cao received an elephant as a gift. He was really delighted and he took his son and officials to have a look at it.

The elephant was huge indeed, with its body like a wall and legs like pillars. The officials discussed how heavy it would be. Cao Cao asked them: "Who can devise a way to weigh the elephant?" One of them answered: "We could have a pair of scales made from a huge tree, or we could kill the elephant and weigh it bit by bit." Another interjected: "A large pair of scales would not work. Who would be strong enough to lift it? And killing it for weighing it? You would know how heavy it is, but there would be no elephant any more!"

Cao Cao shook his head: "Are there any other ideas you can think of?" Cao Cao's son Cao Chong was six at the time. The boy piped up: "I can do it!"

Cao Cao immediately asked him about his plan. Cao Chong said: "Drive the elephant into a large boat and draw a line at the water level. Then drive the elephant back ashore and fill the boat with stones until it sinks in to the marked line. Then weigh the stones and you'll know how heavy the elephant is."

Cao Cao was delighted: "That is a good way to do it." He called upon his men to do as his son had said, and they soon accomplished the weighing of the elephant. All the officials turned red in the face, looking at each other and feeling that they were not even as good as a six-year-old boy.

## Cao Chong

Cao Chong (196-208) was Cao Cao's son. He was bright and affectionate, and Cao Cao was very fond of him. When he was six years old, Cao Chong devised a way to weigh an elephant. He also frequently helped others. Once mice gnawed at some of Cao Cao's things, and the servant in charge was so frightened that he broke into tears. Cao Chong saw this, ripped holes into his own clothes and went to tell his father that the mice had done this. Under the impression that mice had become an uncontrollable plague, Cao Cao did not punish the servant. Cao Chong died of illness when he was only thirteen. Cao Cao was heartbroken.

## I Come from the Han Dynasty

When you check for the character "汉" in the Chinese dictionary, you will find a lot of terms: the Han Dynasty, Chinese characters, the Han Chinese, the Han nationality, the Chinese language, Chinese studies, the River Han, and many more, all starting with "汉". Why?

Liu Bang founded the Han Dynasty in 206 BC, and this dynasty lasted for four centuries. The Han Dynasty was the early period of the Han-Chinese as a nation, and just as young people, who are full of energy and creativity. The people in the Han period created their culture, developed their economy, and expanded their territory. Much like the Roman Empire in Europe, the Han Dynasty in East Asia was the period of a formative, unified civilization as well as a powerful state. She positively communicated with foreign countries and started to reach out to the world. From then on, the language spoken in China came to be called "汉语", the "language of Han"; the characters written in China were called "汉字", the "Chinese character"; and its people called "汉族", "the people of Han".

# 第二课

## 田忌赛马

　　齐国的大将田忌喜欢赛马。有一回他和齐威王比赛。他们把各自的马分成上、中、下三等。比赛的时候，田忌用自己的上等马对齐王的上等马，用中等马对齐王的中等马，用下等马对齐王的下等马。由于齐威王每个等级的马都比田忌的强，三场比赛下来，田忌都输了。他垂头丧气，正要离开赛马场，他的好朋友孙膑(bìn)过来说："从刚才的比赛看，大王的马比你的快不了多少呀……你再同他赛一次，我有办法让你赢。"田忌问孙膑："你是说再换几匹马？"孙膑胸有成竹地说："一匹也不用换。你就照

薛智广　画

我的主意办吧。"

齐威王正在得意洋洋地夸自己的马,看见田忌和孙膑走过来,便说:"怎么,难道你失败了还不服气?"田忌说:"当然不服气,咱们再赛一次!"齐威王说:"那就来吧!"

一声锣响,赛马又开始了。孙膑让田忌先用下等马对齐威王的上等马,第一场输了。第二场,孙膑让田忌拿上等马对齐威王的中等马,赢了第二场。第三场田忌拿中等马对齐威王的下等马,又赢了一场。这下,田忌赢两场输一场,赢了齐威王。还是原来的马,只调换了一下出场顺序,就可转败为胜。

### 田忌赛马

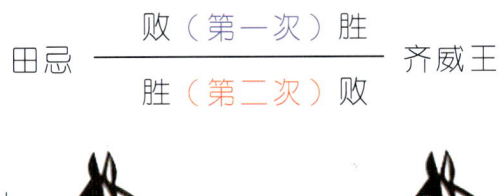

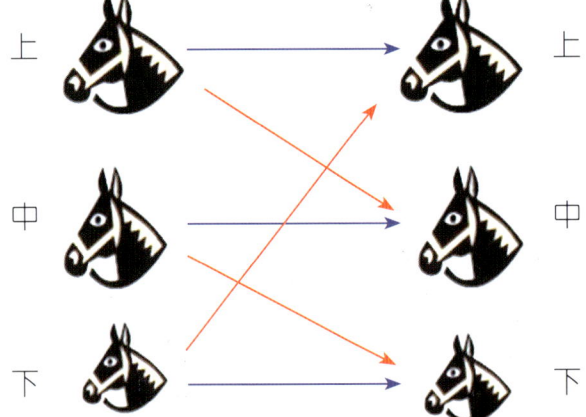

## 资料

① 孙膑，战国时期军事家，孙武的后代。因受害身体残疾。后为齐国军师，帮田忌两次大败庞涓(juān)。

② 田忌，战国时期齐国著名将军。

③ 齐威王（约前378—前320），战国时期齐国君主。

## 生词

| | | | |
|---|---|---|---|
| 忌 jì | first name; envy | 失败 shī bài | be defeated |
| 赛 sài | race; game | 锣 luó | gong |
| 大将 dà jiàng | general | 第一场 dì yī chǎng | the first round |
| 各自 gè zì | each | 赢 yíng | win |
| 等级 děng jí | grade | 调换 diào huàn | exchange |
| 输 shū | lose | 顺序 shùn xù | order |
| 垂头丧气 chuí tóu sàng qì | be dejected | 转败为胜 zhuǎn bài wéi shèng | turn loss into gain |

## 听写

赛　输　等级　垂头丧气　失败　第一场　调换　顺序　*赢

中国古代故事

## 比一比

胜 { 胜利 / 名胜古迹    赛 { 比赛 / 赛马    顺 { 顺序 / 顺利

## 反义词

输　　赢

强——弱　　　失败——成功　　　输——赢

胜——败　　　垂头丧气——得意洋洋

## 多音字

jiāng
将

jiāng 将 { 将军 / 将来

jiàng
将

jiàng 将 { 大将 / 打麻将

## 词语运用

垂头丧气

① 妹妹英文没考好,整个下午都垂头丧气的。

② 这次篮球比赛我们输了,大家垂头丧气地走回来。

转败为胜

① 这次下棋输了没关系,下次努力定会转败为胜。

② 我们眼看要输了,谁知最后又进了两球转败为胜。

## 词语解释

垂头丧气——低着头,没有精神,很不高兴。

转败为胜——眼看要失败的事情,经过努力变为胜利。

## 思考题

举例说明做事情的顺序很重要

提示:先洗手再吃饭

先做作业再玩

汉画像石　力士图

(《力士图》反映出汉代体育竞技活动，雕刻传神，曾作为国礼送给前国际奥委会主席萨马兰齐先生)

# 中国古代体育运动

中国有一幅著名的汉画像石《力士图》，画面是2,000多年前汉朝体育活动的热闹场景：有人拔树，有人背牛，有人斗虎，有人举鼎，还有人抱着羊和美酒来庆祝比赛。

除此之外，中国古代还有赛马、打马球、武术、踢球（鞠）等体育运动。其中马球\*早在汉朝就已开始。唐代马球风行，上到皇帝下到百姓，无论男女老少，都喜欢打马球和看马球。让人惊叹的是，唐代非常开放，女子身体强健，也和男人一样打马球。唐代铜镜上就留下了女子打马球的动人画面。

---

\*马球运动古代叫"击鞠"。

唐代马球图

唐代铜镜

中国古代故事

English Translation

## Tian Ji and the Horse Race

Tian Ji was a general in the State of Qi and he liked horse-racing. Once, he entered into a competition with King Wei of Qi. They each graded their horses into the best, the middling, and the less strong steeds. Then the king and his general raced their horses of matching grades against each other. Because the king's horses of each grade were faster than his general's, Tian Ji lost every round of the race. He was all dejected and about to leave the racing ground, when his friend Sun Bin whispered: "I just saw the race, and the king's horses are just slightly faster than yours. Let them compete again and I'll have you win." Tian Ji said reluctantly: "You mean I should change some horses?" Sun Bin said: "Not a single one. I'll tell you what to do."

King Wei of Qi was highly pleased and full of praise for his horses, when he saw Tian Ji and Sun Bin approach him. He roared: "You still don't accept your defeat?" Tian Ji said: "Of course not, let's race them again!" The king eagerly agreed.

The gong was struck and the race began. Sun Bin let the general's horses of the lowest grade race the king's best horses, and evidently lost. Then he raced the best horses against the king's middling horses, and won. For the third race he set up the middling horses against the king's weaker horses, and won again.

With the same horses, Tian Ji had won two out of three races. By a simple rearrangement of the groups, Sun Bin had turned defeat into victory.

## Sports in Ancient China

There is a famous relief stone of the Han period that shows "strong men" playing sports two thousand years ago: Pulling up trees, carrying oxen, fighting tigers, lifting up bronze tripods. There are also people holding sheep and wine and cheering in the background.

There were also other sports in ancient China, such as horse racing, polo, martial arts, kick-ball. Polo goes back to the Han period. It was most popular during the Tang, when it was played at court as well as by the common people. by men and women alike, and enjoyed by players and spectators. The Tang society was surprisingly open and liberal. Women also enjoyed, riding on horseback and playing polo just like men. We have pictures of women playing polo on bronze mirrors of the Tang Dynasty.

# 第三课

## 李寄杀蛇

汉朝时，南方一座山中有一条很大的毒蛇，经常出来伤人。官府派人杀蛇，不但没有杀死蛇，去的人反倒让毒蛇吃掉了几个，因此人们都十分害怕这条蛇。

后来巫婆说蛇要吃十二三岁的女孩儿。官府只好出钱买女孩儿，由巫婆送到蛇洞口。已经有一些女孩儿活活被蛇吃掉了。

有个女孩儿叫李寄。她只有十三岁，却胆大过人。她向父母

薛智广　画

提出来要去杀蛇除害，父母死活不同意。她就自己跑到官府说，她想杀蛇为民除害。官府见她是个少女，不同意她去，后来看她一定要去，就同意了。李寄说她要一把最好的宝剑和一只猎狗，于是官府给了她一把宝剑和一只凶猛的猎狗。

李寄回家做了许多饭团，准备到时候用。那天清早，李寄让人把饭团搬到蛇洞口，自己一手握着宝剑，一手拉着猎狗等在洞口。其他人早就跑远了。

不一会儿，毒蛇出现了。这蛇有七八丈长，两只眼睛射出凶光。蛇闻到饭团的香味，张开大口吞吃。这时李寄放出猎狗，猎狗扑向毒蛇咬起来。李寄在毒蛇和猎狗咬斗的时候，一个箭步跳起，高举宝剑向蛇背砍去。蛇回头要咬李寄，猎狗又扑上去咬住了大蛇。大蛇用力甩动身子，想把猎狗甩下来。李寄对准毒蛇的身子、尾巴连砍多剑。大蛇死在洞外。

聪明勇敢的李寄杀死了毒蛇，为民除了害。老百姓为了感谢她，把她的故事编成歌，一直传唱着。

## 生词

| | | | |
|---|---|---|---|
| jì 寄 | first name; mail | jiàn 剑 | sword |
| shā 杀 | kill | liè 猎 | hunting |
| dú 毒 | poisonous | zhàng 丈 | a unit of length (=3⅓ metres) |
| guān fǔ 官府 | local authorities | tūn 吞 | swallow |
| fǎn dào 反倒 | instead | dòu 斗 | fight |
| wū pó 巫婆 | witch | jǔ 举 | hold up |
| dǎn dà 胆大 | audacious | kǎn 砍 | chop |
| chú hài 除害 | rid of scourge | yǒng gǎn 勇敢 | brave |

## 听写

李寄　杀　毒蛇　官府　反倒　除害　举剑　猎　吞　勇敢　砍　*斗

## 比一比

传 { 传说 / 传唱 }　　敢 { 勇敢 / 不敢 }　　府 { 官府 / 政府 }

## 进口歌

"才"字进口成一"团",

"元"字进口逛花"园",

"大"字进口找原"因",

"冬"字进口画"图"画,

"玉"字进口建"国"家,

"员"字进口大团"圆"。

## 词语运用

**反倒**

① 雨不但没停,反倒越下越大。

② 医生不常来,母亲的病反倒好些了。

**勇敢**

① 李寄是个勇敢的女孩儿。

② 他勇敢地冲入火场,救出一个小孩儿。

# 标点符号
（biāo fú hào）

中国古代文书（文言文）一般不加标点符号，而是通过语感、语气助词（yán）（bān）等方法断句。这样，有时意思不准。

有这样的笑话，一个无标点句，断句不同，意思也不同。

## 笑话一

无标点句： 下雨天留客天留我不留

断句（1）：下雨天，留客天，留我不？留！（主人留客）

断句（2）：下雨，天留客，天留我不留。（主人不留客）

## 笑话二

无标点句：水龙头不要用坏了

断句（1）：水龙头不要用坏了。

（2）：水龙头不要用，坏了！

# 标点符号介绍（一）

| 名称 | 符号 | 用法 | 例句 |
|---|---|---|---|
| 句号 | 。 | 表示一个陈述句完了 | ① 北京是中国的首都。<br>② 天气越来越冷了。 |
| 逗(dòu)号 | ， | 表示句中停顿 | ① 一声锣响，赛马开始了。<br>② 不久，蚕宝宝长大了。 |
| 叹号 | ！ | 用于感叹句<br>用于语气强烈的祈(qí)使句 | ① 这里的风景太美了！<br>② 停车！ |
| 冒(mào)号 | ： | 用在称呼(hū)后边，提起下文<br>用于引起下文 | ① 亲爱的妈妈：您好！<br>② 他说："原来是你！" |
| 引号 | " " | 表示直接引(jiē)用的部分 | ① 小红说："我一定来。"<br>② 妈妈问："谁来了？" |

读一读，注意标点符号，并用红笔描出：

1. 野骆驼和大熊猫都是珍稀动物。

2. 这下，田忌赢两场，输一场，赢了齐王。

3. 田忌说："当然不服气，咱们再赛一次！"

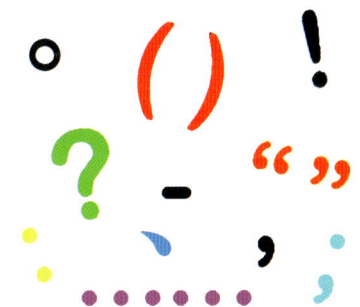

顺口溜(liū)

标点符号很重要，写文章可少不了(liǎo)。

意思未完用逗号，一句完了用句号。

喜怒(nù)哀(āi)乐感叹号，提出问题用问号。

并列(liè)词语用顿号，并列分句用分号。

提示下文用冒号，对话引用加引号。

有些意思要省略(lüè)，可以加上省略号。

标点符号用得对，文章清楚真正好。

# Li Ji Killed the Snake

In the Han period, there was a huge poisonous snake that lived in a mountain in Southern China and often attacked people. The government sent out men to kill the snake. Not only did they fail to kill the snake but several of them actually got eaten by it. Therefore, people grew even more fearful. Later, a witch said the snake wanted to eat young girls who were twelve to thirteen. The officials saw no other way; they bought girls, and the witch took them to the cave where the snake lived.

Several girls were actually eaten by the snake.

There was a girl called Li Ji. She was only thirteen, but she had more courage than anyone else. She told her parents she would go out and get rid of the terrible snake. Her parents totally opposed, so she went to the local government to ask for permission. The officials would not agree, seeing that she was only a young girl. But Li Ji persisted, so they let her go in the end. She said she needed an excellent sword and a hunting dog. The officials gave her the best bronze sword and the fiercest hunting dog.

Li Ji returned home and prepared lots of rice balls. Early in the morning, she set out and had people carry the rice balls up to the cave and scatter them all around. Then everyone ran away, while she stood there with her sword and her dog.

She didn't have to wait long. The snake soon came out. It was 70 to 80 zhang (I zhang equals 3.33 metres) long and had an evil glare in its eyes. Smelling the fragrant rice balls, it opened its huge mouth to swallow them. At this moment, Li Ji let the dog off, and the dog and the snake immediately started biting and fighting. When the two animals were going for each other's head, Li Ji sprang out as fast as an arrow flying from a bow, raised the sword and cut down at the snake's back. The snake turned around to bite, but the dog jumped, caught it, and held it down. The snake writhed to shake off the dog, but Li Ji was faster and hacked away until the snake died outside its cave. Smartly and bravely, Li Ji had freed the people of a dire threat. Her bravery was not forgotten and became a song that was passed down through the generations.

# Chinese Punctuations

Ancient Chinese is usually written without punctuations. You have to use your feeling of rhythm, and marker characters to tell where a sentence ends and the next begins. At times, the meaning is not clear. There are jokes that use the possibilities of creating different meanings by different punctuations.

Joke 1

The sentence without punctuation: 下雨天留客天留我不留

Possibility 1: 下雨天，留客天，留我不？留！

A rainy day is a day to stop a guest from leaving. Does he make me stay? He does!

Possibility 2: 下雨，天留客；天留我不留。

Raining means that heaven stops a guest from leaving. Heaven would make him stay, but I do not.

Joke 2

The sentence without punctuation: 水龙头不要用坏了

Possibility 1: 水龙头不要用坏了。 Don't use the tap in a way that breaks it.

Possibility 2: 水龙头不要用，坏了！ Don't use the tap, it's broken!

# 第四课

## 晏(yàn)子使楚

春秋时期齐国和楚国都是大(dà)国。有一回,齐王派大夫晏子出使楚国。楚王听说晏子很会说话,就想为难为难他。

楚王知道晏子个子矮小,就叫人在城门旁边开了一个五尺(chǐ)高的小门。晏子来到楚国,楚王叫人关上城门,让晏子从这个小门进去。晏子看了看说:"这是个狗洞,不是城门,只有访问'狗国'才从狗洞进去。"话传到楚王那里,楚王只好让人打开城门把晏子迎接进去。

晏子进宫见了楚王,楚王冷冷地说:"难道齐国没有人了吗?"晏子说:"我国首都的人都把袖子举起来,就能连成一片云;大家都甩一把汗,就能下一阵雨;街上的行人一个跟着一个。大王怎么说齐国没有人呢?"楚王说:"既然有这么多人,为什么让你来呢?"晏子说:"我国有个规矩:访问上等的国家，就派上等人去；访问下等的国家，就派下等人去。我最不中用，就派到这儿来了。"楚王听了只好苦笑。

一天，楚王和晏子一起喝酒。正喝得高兴时，见两个卫士带着一个犯人走过。楚王问："那人犯的什么罪？是哪里人？"卫士说："是强盗，齐国人。"楚王嘲笑地对晏子说："齐国人怎么能干这种事情？"楚国的大臣们也跟着笑了。晏子站起来说："大王可听说过，淮(huái)南的橘子，又大又甜。可是这种树一种到淮北，就只能结又小又苦的枳(zhǐ)*，这是因为水土不同。同样的道理，齐国人在齐国能安居乐业好好儿劳动，一到楚国，就做起强盗来了，也许是两国的水土不同吧。"楚王听了说："我原来想取笑大夫，没想到反让大夫取笑了。"

薛智广　画

———————
＊枳——一种味道酸苦的果实。

中国古代故事

## 生词

| | | | |
|---|---|---|---|
| chū shǐ 出使 | be sent on a diplomatic mission | guī ju 规矩 | rule |
| ǎi xiǎo 矮小 | short | fàn rén 犯人 | prisoner, criminal |
| páng biān 旁边 | beside | fàn zuì 犯罪 | commit a crime |
| fǎng wèn 访问 | visit | qiáng dào 强盗 | robber |
| yíng jiē 迎接 | welcome | jú zi 橘子 | orange |
| xiù zi 袖子 | sleeve | ān jū lè yè 安居乐业 | live and work in peace and contentment |
| jì rán 既然 | since | qǔ xiào 取笑 | ridicule, make fun of |

## 听写

出使　矮小　旁边　访问　迎接　袖子　既然　规矩

橘子　安居乐业　取笑　＊犯罪

## 比一比

传
- 传话
- 传唱

楚
- 楚国
- 清楚

转
- 转动
- 转来转去

迎
- 迎接
- 欢迎

## 词语运用

**既然**

① 你**既然**知道错了，就应当马上改正。

② **既然**你一定要去，我也不拦(lán)你了。

③ 你**既然**不喜欢这个电影，为什么还来看？

## 词语解释

不中用——没有用。

安居乐业——安定地生活，愉快地工作。

为难——感到困难，难以应付。

# 标点符号介绍（二）

| 名称 | 符号 | 用法 | 例句 |
|---|---|---|---|
| 问号 | ？ | 用于疑问句 | ① 你喜欢这个餐馆吗？<br>② 飞机怎么飞起来的？ |
| 顿号 | 、 | 用于句中并列词语之间的停顿 | 书包里有书、本、铅笔和橡皮。 |
| 分号 | ； | 表示句中并列分句之间的停顿 | 火车上的人，有的是回家过年；有的是外出旅游的。 |
| 省略号 | …… | 表示文中省略部分 | 山上有桃树、梨树、苹果树…… |

读一读，注意标点符号并用红笔描出：

1. 小燕子叫起来："小山雀，你怎么吃树皮呀？"

2. 中国有长江、黄河、黑龙江、珠江等许多大河。

3. 访问上等的国家，就派上等人去；访问下等的国家，就派下等人去。

4. 中国有汉族、回族、蒙古族、藏族……共56个民族。

## 阅读

### 南橘北枳

橘树种在淮南就是橘，而种在淮北却成了枳。

表示同样的事物，会因环境不同而发生改变（huán）。

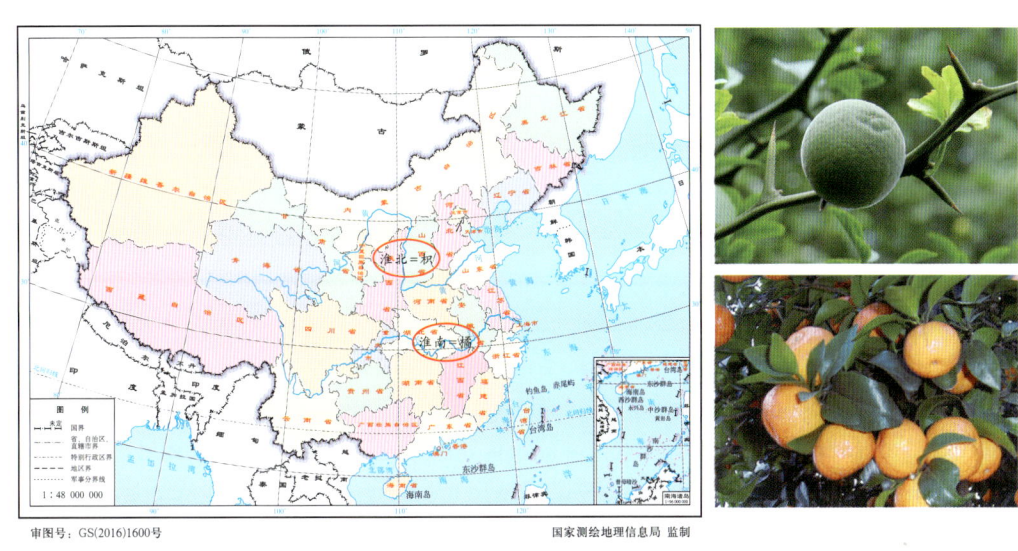

### 没有规矩不成方圆

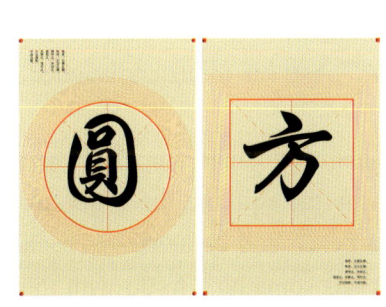

从前鲁班教他的徒弟做圆台和方台，但徒弟怎么也做不圆，造不方。鲁班笑着给他两样东西。一会儿，徒弟就用木头做出了圆台和方台。原来那两件东西就是规和矩（lǔ）：规是圆规，用来画圆；矩是折尺，可画出直线、直角和量长度。

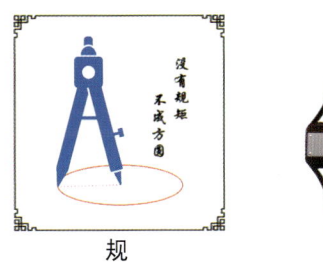
规

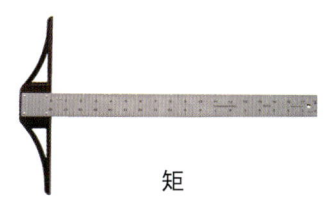
矩

## Yanzi on a Mission to Chu

In the Chunqiu period the largest states were Qi and Chu, and the King of Qi once sent Yanzi on a mission to Chu. The King of Chu had heard that Yanzi was particularly eloquent, and he wanted to put him on the spot.

He knew also that Yanzi was a very small man. Therefore, he called upon his men to open small door next to the main city gate, only 5 chi (about I meter) high. When Yanzi arrived, he had the main gate closed so that Yanzi would have to enter the city by the small gate. Yanzi took a look and said: "This is the entrance to a dog kennel, not a city gate. Only if you wanted to get to the city of dogs would you enter by this gate." When this was reported to the King, he had no choice but to open the main gate and welcome Yanzi.

Yanzi came to the palace to have an audience with the King of Chu, who said coldly: "How come there's nobody left in the State of Qi?" Yanzi answered: "If everyone in our capital threw up their sleeves, it would look like a cloud floating above the city, and if all wiped their sweat at the same time, it would be like a shower of rain. People in the streets move in throngs. Why would your majesty say there is nobody left in Qi?" The King said: "Since there are so many people, how come you were sent here?" Yanzi said: "We have this rule: For missions to high-ranking states, a high-ranking person is sent; and for low-ranking states a low-ranking person. Now I'm the most useless of all, so I was sent here." All the King of Chu could do was to put on a forced smile.

Sometime later, the King and Yanzi were drinking together. When they were just enjoying themselves, two guards passed by escorting a prisoner. The King called out: "What crime has he committed? Where is he from?" The guards answered: "He is a robber and from the State of Qi." The King laughed and turned to Yanzi: "Are people from Qi really like this?" And his ministers laughed, too. Yanzi got up.

"Great King, you would have heard how big and sweet the oranges of Huainan are. But when you transplant them to Huaibei, they turn bitter and sour. This is because the soil and the water are different. It is the same with the people of Qi. They live and work in peace and contentment back home, but when they come to Chu, they turn into robbers. I suppose it has something to do with the soil and the water." When the King of Chu heard this, he said: "Counsellor, I wanted to ridicule you, but I had not expected to be ridiculed by you."

## The Oranges of the South and the Sour Fruit of the North

The saying "the orange trees planted in Huainan bear oranges but planted in Huaibei bear only sour fruit" means that the same thing may turn out different in a different environment.

# No Square or a Circle without Straight-edge and Compass

In ancient times, Lu Ban taught his apprentice how to make square and round platforms. But no matter how hard the apprentice tried, his platforms were neither square nor round. Lu Ban laughed and gave him two things. Soon afterwards, the apprentice was able to make both square and round platforms. The two things were the compass for drawing circles, and the straight-edge for drawing straight lines, right angles, and for measuring length!

# 第五课

## 西门豹的故事

战国时期，魏王派西门豹去管理邺(yè)这个地方。西门豹到了那里一看，人口很少，土地没人种，就问一位老人是怎么回事。老人说："都是因为河神娶亲。漳(zhāng)河的神，每年要娶个漂亮的姑娘。要是不给他送，漳河就要发大水，把田地全淹了。"

西门豹问："这是谁说的？"老人说："巫婆说的。官绅每年都给河神办喜事，硬让老百姓出钱。办喜事多出来的钱就跟巫婆分了。"西门豹又问："新娘是哪儿来的？"老人说："哪家有年轻的女孩子，巫婆就到哪家去选。有钱的人家花点儿钱就过

薛智广 画

去了；没钱的只好眼看着女儿被拉走。到了河神娶亲那天，他们让打扮好的女孩儿坐在草席上，顺着水漂去。到了河中心，草席连女孩儿一起沉下去了。有女儿的人家都逃走了。"西门豹想了想说："下次河神娶亲，告诉我一声，我也去送送新娘。"

到了河神娶亲的日子，漳河边上站满了老百姓。西门豹带着卫士真的来了。巫婆和当地的官绅急忙迎接。西门豹说："把新娘领来让我看看。"巫婆领来新娘，西门豹一看，女孩儿满脸泪水。他说："不行，这个姑娘不漂亮，河神不会满意的。请你去跟河神说一声，我选个漂亮的，过几天送去。"说完，叫卫士抱起巫婆扔进了漳河。巫婆在河里扑腾(téng)了几下，沉下去了。等了一会儿，西门豹对官绅的头子说："巫婆怎么还不回来？你去催一催吧。"说完，又叫卫士把官绅的头子也扔进了漳河。

西门豹面对着漳河站了很久。那些官绅都吓得面如土色，跪下求饶。西门豹说："起来吧。看样子是河神把他们留下了。你们都回去吧。"老百姓都明白了，巫婆和官绅都是骗钱害人的。

西门豹带领老百姓开水渠，把漳河的水引到田里。每年的收成都很好。从那以后，漳河再也没有发过大水。老百姓从此安居乐业。

## 生词

| | | | |
|---|---|---|---|
| bào 豹 | leopard | xīn niáng 新娘 | bride |
| wèi 魏 | Wei State | xuǎn 选 | choose |
| guǎn lǐ 管理 | manage | dǎ ban 打扮 | dress up |
| qǔ qīn 娶亲 | take a wife | cǎo xí 草席 | straw mat |
| yān 淹 | flood, submerge | cuī 催 | hasten, urge |
| guān shēn 官绅 | officer | qiú ráo 求饶 | beg for mercy |
| yìng 硬 | force | shuǐ qú 水渠 | ditch; aqueduct |

## 听写

魏　管理　娶亲　淹　硬　选　打扮　草席　催　水渠　*求饶

## 比一比

{ 取（取笑） / 娶（娶亲） }　　　　{ 危（危险） / 跪（跪下） }

## "席"字的演变

席：用草、竹子等编的成片的东西，用来坐卧(wò)。

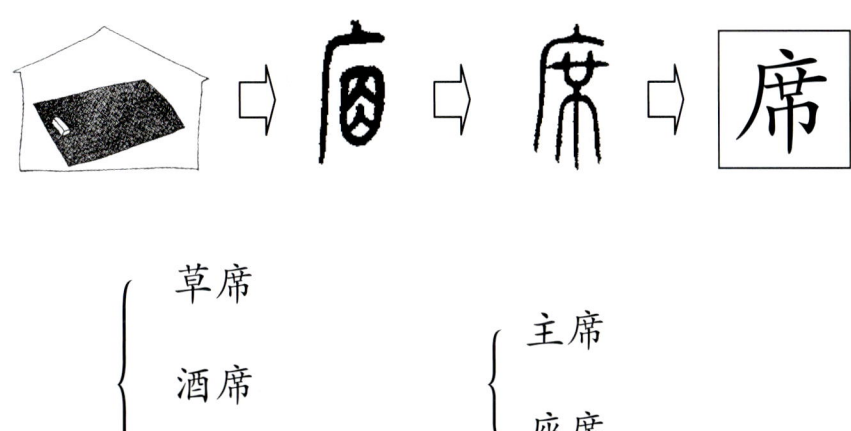

草席
酒席
竹席

主席
座席

## 反义词

硬——软　　本地——外地　　迎接——欢送

高——矮　　胆大——胆小　　喜事——丧(sāng)事

## 多音字

piāo　　　　　　　　piào
漂　　　　　　　　　漂
漂走　　　　　　　　漂亮

## 词语运用

遍　骗　编

① 这个电影我已经看过两遍了。

② 狐狸骗乌鸦说:"你有五彩的羽毛，真漂亮!"

③ 我过生日，姐姐编了一本小画书送给我，我可喜欢了。

满意

① 小华数学考试得了A，他很满意。

② 西门豹说:"新娘不漂亮，河神不会满意的。"

③ 这件衣服很漂亮，你满意吗?

## 词语解释

发大水——下雨太多，江河湖中的水流出来。

官绅——官员和当地有钱、有名的人。

喜事——使人高兴的事，特指结婚(hūn)。

收成——稻子、麦子、棉花、蔬菜、水果等农作物的产量。

满意——心愿得到满足。

# 西门豹（课本剧）

人物：西门豹、老大爷、巫婆、新娘、官绅、百姓、卫士等

旁白：战国时期，西门豹去管理邺，他找了位老大爷打听情况。

西门豹：老大爷，这儿人口很少，没人种地，为什么呢？

老大爷：都是因为河神娶亲！漳河的神，每年要娶个漂亮姑娘。要不然就发大水。

西门豹：这是谁说的？

老大爷：巫婆说的。每年官绅都给河神办喜事，让老百姓出钱。用不完的钱就跟巫婆分了。

西门豹：新娘是哪儿来的？

老大爷：哪家有年轻的女孩儿，巫婆就到哪家去。河神娶亲那天，女孩儿坐在草席上顺水漂去，没多久就沉下去了，所以有女孩儿的人家都逃走了。

西门豹：下次河神娶亲，告诉我一声，我也去送送新娘子。（讽刺fěng）

旁白：到了河神娶亲的日子，西门豹真的带着卫士来了，巫婆、官绅急忙迎接。

西门豹：把新娘子领来我看看。（傲ào慢）

新娘子（满脸泪水）：拜见西门大人。

西门豹：（皱zhòu着眉头对巫婆说）这个新娘子不好看，河神不会满意的。你去跟河神说一声，我要选一个更漂亮的，过几天送去。（对卫士）来呀，把她扔下去。

巫婆：救命啊！救命啊！……（卫士驾jià着退场）

（过了一会儿）

西门豹：巫婆怎么还没回来？（对官绅头子）请你去催一下。

（对卫士）来呀，把他扔下去。

官绅头子：大人饶命啊……（卫士驾着退场）

众官绅：（连忙下跪）西门大人饶命啊……

西门豹：起来吧。看样子是河神把他们留下了。

旁白：老百姓都明白了，巫婆和官绅都是骗钱害人的。西门豹带领老百姓，开水渠，把漳河的水引到田里，年年都有好收成。从此人们安居乐业。

# The Story of Ximen Bao

In the Warring States period, the King of Wei sent Ximen Bao to rule over Ye. Ximen Bao arrived at Ye and saw immediately that there were few people and much untilled land. He asked an old man for the reason. The old man said: "It's all because the God of the Zhang River takes a new wife every year. Every year, we have to offer him a pretty girl, otherwise he would cause a flood and inundate all our fields."

Ximen Bao asked: "Who told you that?" The old man answered: "The witch. The local dignitaries hold a wedding for the River God every year, and we common people have to pay for it all. Any money left over is shared by the dignitaries and the witch." Ximen Bao asked: "And where does the bride come from?" The old man answered: "If any family has a young girl, the witch might come and take her. People who have money can bribe to let their daughters go, those who don't would have their girl taken away. On the wedding day, the girl has to dress up as a bride and sit on a straw mat, then she is pushed out onto the river, and as she reaches the middle, the mat and the girl go under. The families who have girls all run away." Ximen Bao thought for a while and said: "Let me know when the next wedding is to be held, I want to send a bride as well."

On the wedding day of the River God, when the bank of the River Zhang was crowded with people, Ximen Bao also arrived with his guardsmen. The witch and the local dignitaries rushed forth to greet him. Ximen Bao said: "Show me the bride." The witch brought the bride and Ximen Bao saw that the girl was in tears. He said: "This won't do, the girl is too ugly, the River God won't like her. Please go and tell him. I'll find a pretty bride and we will have the wedding in a few days." Upon which the guards grabbed the witch and threw her into the River Zhang. The witch struggled for a bit and sank. They waited for a while, then Ximen Bao spoke to the leader of the dignitaries: "Why is she taking so long? Go and tell her to hurry up, please." Whereupon the guards threw him into the river as well.

Ximen Bao stood at the river and looked out for a long time. The other dignitaries were so frightened that their faces had taken the colour of mud, they knelt down and begged for mercy. Ximen Bao said: "Get up. I think the River God asked them to stay. We can all go home." This is when all the people understood that they had been cheated by the witch and the dignitaries.

Ximen Bao then led the commoners to open a canal that diverted the water of the River Zhang to irrigate their fields. From then on, the people enjoyed good harvests year after year, and the River Zhang no longer flooded the area. The people lived in peace and enjoyed the fruit of their labours.

# 第六课

## 张良拜师

张良是秦汉时期的人，汉朝的开国功臣。张良原是韩国人，韩国被秦所灭，张良一心想刺杀秦始皇，结果没成功，只好躲在乡下。

一天，他正在桥上走，看见一位白胡子老人坐在桥头。老人见张良过来，把脚一伸，鞋掉到了桥下。老人对张良说："喂，小伙子，下去把我的鞋捡上来。"张良听了很吃惊，心想：真不懂礼貌！可又一想：老人胡子都白了，就帮他吧。于是下桥把鞋子拾起来。当张良恭恭敬敬地把鞋子给他时，老人反而把脚一伸说："帮我穿上。"张良真想发火，但还是忍住了，想：年轻人给老人干点儿活，有什么不好呢？他给老人穿上了。老人笑笑，一句感谢的话都没说就走了。

张良觉得奇怪，就一直跟在老人后面。走了一里地，老人回过头对张良说："你这个小伙子还不错，心地善良，又有耐心，我可以教导教导你。这样吧，五天后天亮的时候，你到桥上来见我。"张良知道碰上了高人，连忙跪下回答："是，先生。"

第五天，天刚亮张良就起床赶到桥头，谁知道老人已经等在那里了。他见到张良，生气地说："年轻人，跟老人约会，就该早点儿来，怎么叫我等你呢？"张良连忙跪下认错。老人说："今天算了，再过五天早一点儿来。"说完，头也不回就走了。

五天后，张良没等天亮，就急急忙忙向桥头走去，谁知道还没上桥，就看见老人又等在那里了。张良刚想道歉，老人瞪了张良一眼说："不用说了，过五天再来。"

五天时间很快就过了四天。第四天夜里，张良不敢睡觉，在屋子里走来走去。刚过半夜，张良就赶到桥头。这次，他终于赶在老人前面了。一会儿，老人来了，高兴地说："这就对了。"

薛智广　画

 中国古代故事

老人拿出一部书给张良，说："这书非常珍贵，送给你，回去好好儿读，将来一定能成大事。我等你的好消息。"

张良回去一看，原来是著名的《太公兵法》。此后，张良用心读书，懂得了用兵之道。几年后，张良帮助刘bāng邦推翻了秦朝，建立了汉朝。

## 生词

| | | | |
|---|---|---|---|
| bài shī 拜师 | acknowledge sb. as one's master | shí 拾 | pick up |
| gōng chén 功臣 | hero | gōng jìng 恭敬 | respectfully |
| hán 韩 | Han State | nài xīn 耐心 | patience |
| miè 灭 | destroy | jiàodǎo 教导 | instruct |
| cì shā 刺杀 | assassinate | yuē huì 约会 | make an appointment |
| chī jīng 吃惊 | be shocked | dào qiàn 道歉 | apologize |
| dǒng 懂 | know | tuī fān 推翻 | overthrow |
| lǐ mào 礼貌 | courtesy, polite | | |

## 听写

拜师　韩　灭　刺杀　吃惊　礼貌　懂　恭敬　耐心　约会　推翻　*道歉

## 比一比

约 { 约会　大约 }　　敬 { 恭敬　尊敬 }

导 { 教导　导游 }　　懂 { 听懂　懂事 }

## 词语运用

**道歉**

① 这么长时间了才给他回信，真该道歉。

② 华明红着脸道歉说："对不起，我来晚了。"

**恭敬**

① 张良恭恭敬敬地把鞋给了老人。

② 爸爸对他的老师很恭敬。

### 重叠形容词,读一读并记住:

恭敬——恭恭敬敬　　暖和——暖暖和和
高兴——高高兴兴　　明白——明明白白
干净——干干净净　　大方——大大方方

- 窗外下着鹅毛大雪,可屋子里暖暖和和的。
- 小妹妹只有8岁,可是上台唱歌却大大方方的。
- 哥哥的作业总是写得干干净净的。
- 门上明明白白写着四个大字"今天休息"。
- 下课了,同学们在院子里高高兴兴地玩儿球。
- 张良恭恭敬敬地把鞋给老人。

## 阅读

### 张良的老师——黄石公

张良拜师的故事中，有位老人给了张良一本书——《太公兵法》，告诉他："读了这本书，能成大事。13年后，你会在济北遇到我，谷城山下有块黄石就是我。"张良得到《太公兵法》后，用心读书，有了本领，帮助刘邦建立了汉朝。13年后，张良路过济北，果真在谷城山下看见一块黄石。张良取回它，把它当作珍宝。张良死后，就和这块黄石埋在一起。后来，张良和老师黄石公的故事被写在《史记》里。

黄石公像

### 资料

张良，秦末汉初人。出身韩国贵族，祖父、父亲曾是韩国宰相。张良曾刺杀秦始皇失败，后帮助刘邦建立汉朝，是汉朝的功臣。

## 摸　钟

　　古时候，有位聪明的县官。一天，有人说家里被偷了。县官很快抓来几个人，但他们都说自己没偷。县官想了一个办法。城外古庙里有一口大钟。当时的老百姓都相信这大钟很神，能认出贼(zéi)。

　　县官把他们带到古庙，向大钟行了礼，然后说："现在，你们一个一个走进屋里去摸钟。没偷东西的，摸钟时，钟不会响；要是偷了东西，一摸钟，钟就会响。"人们轮(lún)流摸完了钟，大钟一直没有声音。大家以为没事，可以回去了。县官说："大家把手伸出来让我看看。"好多人的手都黑了，只有一个人的手是干净的。县官大声说："东西是你偷的！"那人吓了一跳，说："老爷，不是我。"县官笑着说："大钟怎么会认贼(zéi)呢！是我在钟上涂了墨。没偷东西的人，放心摸钟，手就会黑。只有你偷了东西，不敢摸钟，两只手自然是干净的了。"这个人听了，马上跪在地上认罪(zuì)。

薛智广　画

 English Translation

# Zhang Liang Found a Teacher

Zhang Liang lived during the transition from the Qin to the Han and became a minister of great merit under the early Han. He was originally from the State of Han, and when the Han was annihilated by the Qin, he swore to assassinate the First Emperor. He failed, however, and had to hide in the countryside.

One day, he came to a bridge and saw a man with a white beard sitting there. When the man saw Zhang Liang coming near, he stretched out his leg and his shoe dropped off the bridge. He called out to Zhang Liang: "Hey, young man, get my shoe back, will you?" Zhang Liang was rather surprised and thought: "He is so rude!" But then he thought again: "He is old and his beard is all white, let me help him." So he climbed down the bridge and picked up the shoe. When he presented it politely, the old man stretched out his leg and said: "Put it on for me." Zhang Liang almost got angry, but he kept it down, thinking: "The young should help the elderly, nothing wrong with that." He put the shoe on the foot of the old man, who laughed and left without even saying "Thank you."

Zhang Liang thought this rather strange, so he followed the old man. They walked for one Li, then the old man turned around and said: "You are a nice young man. You have kindness and patience. I could give you some instructions well. Come back in five days at the break of day and I'll see you at the bridge." Zhang Liang realized that he had just met a man of great wisdom. He immediately knelt down and said: "Yes, sir."

On the fifth day, Zhang Liang got up and hastened to the bridge at the break of day. Who would have thought the old man was already waiting there! Upon seeing Zhang Liang, he said angrily: "Young man, if you have an appointment with an old man, you'd better come early. How come you let me wait?" Zhang Liang knelt down and acknowledged his fault. The old man said: "Let's forget about today, come earlier in five days." With this, he turned around and left. Five days later, Zhang Liang hastened to the bridge before dawn, yet even before getting there, he realized that the old man was already waiting. He didn't even wait for Zhang Liang's apologies, but glared at him: "You don't need to waste words, come back in five days." On the night of the fourth day, Zhang Liang did not dare to sleep, but paced up and down his room and set out just after midnight. This time, he finally got there before the old man did. After a little while, he turned up and said happily: "Well done!"

The old man took out a book and gave it to Zhang Liang: "This book is precious, take it as my gift. If you study it diligently, you will achieve great deeds. I will await your good news." Zhang Liang took the book home and found out it was the famous *Lord Jiang's Military Strategems*. Zhang Liang studied the book and understood the way of war. Several years later, he helped Liu Bang overthrow the Qin dynasty and found the Han.

# Zhang Liang's Teacher-Master Yellow Stone

In the story of Zhang Liang, there was an old man giving a book to Zhang Liang, the *Lord Jiang's Military Strategems*, and saying: "If you read this book, you will achieve great deeds. In thirteen years, you will meet me in Jibei, the yellow stone under the Mount Gucheng is me." After obtaining the book, Zhang Liang studied it and gained the capabilities that he used to help Liu Bang in founding the Han dynasty. Thirteen years later, he passed by Jibei, and as expected, found a yellow stone under the Mount Gucheng. Zhang Liang took this stone home and regarded it as a treasure. When he died, he was buried with this yellow stone. The story of Zhang Liang and his teacher, Master Yellow Stone, was later recorded in *Shiji*.

Zhang Liang lived in the late Qin and early Han periods. He was from a noble family of the State of Han, both his grandfather and his father had been prime ministers to the King of Han. Zhang Liang carried out a failed assassination attempt on the First Emperor of the Qin, and later helped Liu Bang in founding the Han. Thus he became a meritorious minister of the Han dynasty.

# Touching the Bell

In ancient times, there was a clever local official. One day, somebody reported that his house had been robbed. The official soon caught several suspects, who all denied having stolen anything. The local official thought of a way to find out the culprit. There was a large bell in an old temple outside the city, and people believed that this bell had magic powers and could identify a thief.

The local official had them all taken to the old temple, where he presented an offering to the bell and said: "Now you go in and touch the bell, one after another. When someone who has not stolen anything touches the bell, it will remain silent, but when a thief touches it, the bell will ring." The suspects went in one after another, and the bell made no sound. They all thought that everything was fine and they could go home. But the official said: "Show me your hands!" They all stretched out their hands, and all hands were blackened, except one guy's hands were clean. The official shouted: "You are the thief!" The man was startled: "Your honor, it isn't me!" The official laughed: "How could a bell identify a thief! It was me who had the bell blacked with ink. Anyone who had a clean conscience would touch the bell, and their hands would get black. Only you, because you had stolen the things, you did not dare to touch it. That is why your hands are clean." Upon hearing this, the man knelt down and admitted his crime.

# 第七课

## 三试华佗(huà tuó)

华佗是三国时期的名医。他发明了麻醉药。

华佗小时候家里很穷，父亲早亡。后来，华佗的母亲又得了怪病，医生治不了，眼看着母亲痛苦地死去。从此，他立志学医救人。

华佗听说有位精通医术的道人，名叫治华。他不怕山高路远，走了一个月，找到了治华道人\*，拜他为师。治华问他："学医很苦，你真的想学吗？"华佗说："我不怕苦，真心，诚心。"治华说："既然你真心，就先照看病人吧。"治华带他来到一个大院子，华佗一看大吃一惊：里面到处躺着病人，腿上流脓(nóng)的，受伤出血的——什么病人都有。治华说："你要烧水，刷盆，照看病人。"华佗二话没说，就干了起来。不论刮风下雨，白天黑夜，他从不离开病人。师父给病人吃什么药，他都一一记

---

\*道人——对道士的尊称。道士是道教的宗教(zōng zhí)职业者。

在心里。

三年过去了，治华把华佗带到书房，里面到处是药书和挂图，说："读书不能心急，你就在这里认真读书吧。"

冬去春来，三年又过去了。华佗读书从不偷懒。一天晚上，华佗正在看书，有人跑来说："师父病重，你快去看看吧。"华佗赶去一看，师父躺在床上，谁也不知道他得了什么病。华佗走到床头给师父摸了一下脉，笑着说："大家放心，师父没病。"这时治华道人坐起来说："我的确没病，是试试你们的。"大家非常佩服华佗。

正说话时，忽然书房着火了，大家冲进去救火，可是晚了，许多书被烧成了灰。众师兄非常心痛。华佗想：幸好自己把医书都背熟了，可以默写出来。于是他开始默写医书。许多天过去了，他终于把烧掉的医书都默写出来了。

薛智广　画

当他把这件事告诉师父时,治华笑着说道:"那火是我让人点的。不过烧掉的不是医书,只想考考你书读得怎样了。现在你真的学成了,通过了三次考试,我不再留你了。"

华佗告别了师父,开始了治病救人的生涯。

## 生词

| | | | |
|---|---|---|---|
| fā míng 发明 | invent | dí què 的确 | indeed |
| má zuì yào 麻醉药 | narcotic | pèi fú 佩服 | admire |
| tòng kǔ 痛苦 | pain | zhòng 众 | many |
| lì zhì 立志 | aspire | xìng hǎo 幸好 | fortunately |
| jīng tōng 精通 | be proficient in | mò xiě 默写 | write from memory |
| yī shù 医术 | art of healing, medical skills | kǎo shì 考试 | test |
| chéng xīn 诚心 | wholeheartedness, sincere desire | gào bié 告别 | say goodbye to |
| mō mài 摸脉 | touch the pulse | shēng yá 生涯 | career, profession |

中国古代故事

## 听写

发明　立志　精通　诚心　的确　佩服　众　幸好

默写　考试　告别　*麻醉药

## 比一比

刷 { 刷盆 / 刷子 }　　诚 { 诚实 / 诚心 }　　幸 { 幸好 / 幸福 }

别 { 别人 / 告别 }　　术 { 医术 / 算术 }　　脉 { 山脉 / 摸脉 }

## 多音字

的　dí
的确

的　de
我的

## 词语运用

的确

① 昆明的天气的确很好,四季如春。

② 北京烤鸭的确好吃。

**幸好**

① <u>幸好</u>路上车少，我们很快就开到旧金山了。

② <u>幸好</u>天下大雪，我们可以去滑雪了。

### 重叠形容词，读一读并记住

清楚——清清楚楚　　平安——平平安安

整齐——整整齐齐　　辛苦——辛辛苦苦

漂亮——漂漂亮亮　　舒服——舒舒服服

◆ 星期日，我舒舒服服地睡了一大觉。

◆ 小花把自己的屋子收拾得整整齐齐的。

◆ 华佗辛辛苦苦地照看病人。

◆ 妈妈希望我们平平安安地回来。

◆ 开学第一天，小红穿得漂漂亮亮的。

◆ 弟弟的作业总是写得清清楚楚。

## 中国古代故事

## 阅读

### 华佗和"麻沸(fèi)散"

华佗(145—208)是三国时期的名医,精通外科(kē)手术,人们称他为"神医"。

但让华佗头痛的是:做手术时病人疼痛难忍。一次,人们抬来一个病人,他喝醉(zuì)酒,摔断了腿。华佗给他做手术,病人烂醉如泥,一点儿看不出痛苦。这让华佗有了新的想法:如果药和酒一起喝下去,人失去知觉就好了。后来,他发明了中药"麻沸散"(麻醉药),让病人用酒服下,全身失去知觉,再做手术,就不痛苦了。华佗是世界上第一个发明麻醉药的人,也是第一个使用全身麻醉方法的医生,比国外要早1,600年。

### 五禽(qín)戏

五禽戏是华佗编的一套健身运动,通过学虎、鹿、熊、猴、鸟的动作,活动身体。他认为运动可以强身,希望人们身体强健,少生病。

## 华佗的故事

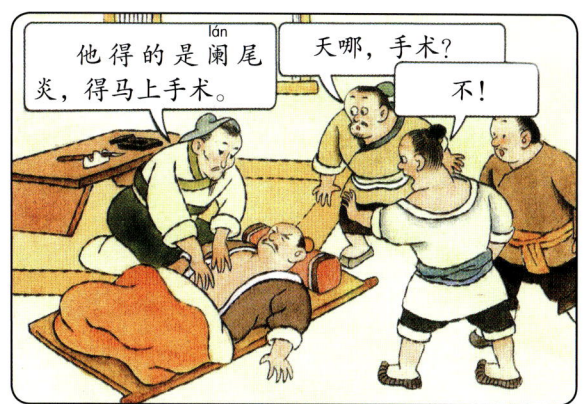

华佗给病人手术，一切顺利

## 华佗和关羽

关羽打仗，手臂中了毒箭。华佗为他做手术，要把他捆在柱子上，再蒙上他的眼睛。关羽说：“不用了，先生只管手术，我和别人下棋便是。”果然，华佗手术，关羽专心下棋，不出一声。华佗惊叹：“将军乃神人也。”

Hong Tao and Feng Congying 画

# The Three Tests for Hua Tuo

Hua Tuo was a famous doctor who lived in the period of the Three Kingdoms. He invented narcotics.

When Hua Tuo was young, his family was very poor and he lost his father at an early age. Later, Hua Tuo's mother contracted a strange illness that the doctor could not cure, and Hua Tuo had to see her die in agony. From that time, he dedicated his life to study medicine in order to save lives. Hua Tuo heard of a Daoist who had a profound understanding of medicine. His name was Zhihua. Without thinking of the height of the mountains or the distance he had to overcome, Hua Tuo travelled for a month and finally met Daoist Zhihua. He greeted him and begged him to be his teacher. Zhihua said: "Studying medicine is very hard. Do you really want to do it?" Hua Tuo answered: "I do not fear hardness, it is my heart's desire." Zhihua said: "Since it truly is your heart's desire, start with looking after patients." He took Hua Tuo into a big courtyard and Hua Tuo was taken aback: it was full of patients with all sorts of afflictions, lying there with ulcers on their legs, bleeding from wounds. Zhihua said: "Boil water, scrub bedpans and tend their wounds." Hua Tuo said nothing but immediately set to work. Came wind or rain, by day and night, he would not leave his patients. And he remembered all his master's prescriptions in his heart.

Three years had passed, when Zhihua took him into his study, which was full of medical books and pictures, he said: "When you study, you have to take your time, stay here and read the books carefully." Winter turned into spring, and again three years passed. Hua Tuo studied diligently. One evening, as he was reading, a servant rushed in: "The master is gravely ill, come quickly!" Hua Tuo found his teacher lying in bed, and nobody knew what his illness was. Hua Tuo hastened to his bedside and took his pulse, then he laughed: "No need to worry, our master is not ill!" Whereupon Zhihua sat up: "I am really not ill, I was just testing you." Everyone was in awe of Hua Tuo.

As they were still talking, a fire broke out in the study. They all rushed to put out the fire, but it was too late. Many medical works had been burnt to ashes. The disciples were crushed by the loss, but Hua Tuo thought to himself: "Fortunately, I memorized all these books and can write them down again from memory." So he began writing the medical books down from memory. It took several days, but he finally replaced all the lost books.

When he told his teacher, Zhihua laughed: "I had that fire lit, but the burnt books actually were not the medicine works. It was just a test to see how well you had studied them. Your studies are now complete, you have passed three tests and I will not keep you here any longer."

Hua Tuo bid his teacher farewell and went out to fulfil his mission of curing and saving people.

# Hua Tuo and the *Mafeisan*

Living in the Three Kingdoms period, Hua Tuo (145-208 AD) was a famous doctor who had profound knowledge of surgery and was called the "godlike doctor". But Hua Tuo was acutely aware of the pain that his patients suffered when he performed operations. Once, a patient who had broken a leg in drunken stupor was brought in. Hua Tuo operated on him. The leg was a mess, yet the man appeared to feel no pain. This gave Hua Tuo an idea: The solution would be a medicine that could be taken with alcohol and make the patient lose the feeling in their body. Later on, he invented the "Mafeisan", a traditional Chinese medicine that was used as narcotics. It was given to patients with alcohol and made them unconscious so that an operation would cause them no pain. Hua Tuo was the first doctor on earth who used general anesthetics.

# Wuqinxi

Wuqinxi ("five animals' play") is a form of exercise that Hua Tuo developed. Imitating movements of tigers, deer, bears, monkeys, and birds, the whole body is activated. The exercise builds strength and helps with staying healthy.

# Hua Tuo and Guan Yu

Guan Yu received a wound in the shoulder during a battle. Hua Tuo was to operate on him. He wanted to tie Guan Yu to a pillar and cover his eyes. Guan Yu said: "That's unnecessary. You do your operation, and I play a game of chess with my men." And indeed, while Hua Tuo performed his operation, Guan Yu was all focused on his game, and never made a sound. Hua Tuo sighed in admiration: "General, you are superhuman."

# 第八课

## 高山流水

中国有一首著名的古曲叫《高山流水》。听《高山流水》,人若在天地间、山水中,物我两忘,天人合一。关于这首古曲,有一段动人的故事流传了2,000多年。

相传战国时,楚国有一位琴师俞伯牙,他琴艺高超。一天晚上,月明风清,伯牙在船上弹琴。琴声悠扬,飘于山川天地之间。弹着弹着,琴弦突然断了。伯牙心想:难道有人在听琴?人们常说,懂音乐又懂琴师心情的人听琴,琴弦就会断。伯牙一看,果然有一位樵夫在听琴。他头戴斗笠,手里拿着一把砍柴的斧头,脚边还有一捆柴,这人叫钟子期。伯牙以为在山野间不会有人真懂得音乐,于是想试试钟子期。伯牙弹了一首《高山》的曲子。乐曲一停,钟子期就说:"好!巍巍兮若泰山!"伯牙又弹了一首《流水》的曲子，音乐从指尖流出，如同滚滚江水。钟子期又说道："好！洋洋兮若江河！"伯牙看钟子期如此知音，非常感动，相见恨晚。于是他们成了好朋友，并约好明年的中秋节再次相见。

第二年伯牙如期到来，却得知钟子期已不在人世。大颗的泪水从伯牙眼中流出。他抱着琴到钟子期坟前，为钟子期弹琴，放声悲歌。而后，伯牙就把心爱的琴摔在石头上，琴断成两半。从此伯牙再也不弹琴了，因为世上已无人能欣赏他美妙的琴声了。

以后，人们就用"高山流水"比喻"知音，知己"。

陈巽如　画

## 中国古代故事

### 生词

| | | | |
|---|---|---|---|
| 若 ruò | seem | 斧头 fǔ tou | axe |
| 琴艺 qín yì | skill in playing stringed instruments | 巍巍 wēi wēi | towering, lofty |
| 高超 gāo chāo | superb | 如此 rú cǐ | like that; so |
| 弹琴 tán qín | play the piano | 知音 zhī yīn | bosom friend |
| 悠扬 yōu yáng | rising and falling | 相见恨晚 xiāng jiàn hèn wǎn | regret not to have known sb. before |
| 飘 piāo | gone with the wind | | |
| 琴弦 qín xián | strings | 欣赏 xīn shǎng | appreciate |
| 一捆柴 yì kǔn chái | a bundle of sticks | 美妙 měi miào | wonderful |

### 听写

高超　弹琴　悠扬　斧头　若　如此　知音

欣赏　美妙　*一捆柴

### 比一比

超 { 高超　超过　超市 }

知 { 知音　知道　知识 }

{ 很（很好）　恨（相见恨晚）　狠（凶狠） }

## 反义词

爱——恨　　　　　忘——记

## 量词练习

一（首）歌　　　　一（捆）柴

一（首）诗　　　　一（捆）草

## 词语运用

**首**

① 表演会上，丽华一连唱了四首歌。

② 这是一首李白的诗。

**如此**

① 小提琴曲《梁祝》如此之美，大家都很喜欢。

② 姐姐如此快乐，是因为她进入了学校游泳队。

③ 弟弟如此着急，因为他的小兔子丢了。

## 词语解释

月明风清——月光明朗,微风清爽,美好的夜晚。

相见恨晚——认识得太晚了。

## 阅读

### 高山流水

《高山流水》原为古琴曲,是中国音乐艺术的珍品。它赞(zàn)美琴师俞伯牙与听琴人钟子期,由知音而成为生死朋友,意在感叹"知音难求"。全曲立意清高,有气势,有形象。建议大家在中国旅游时,也听听这首古曲。

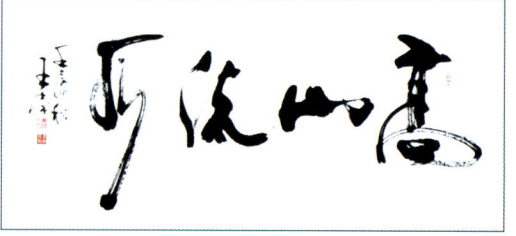

# 敦煌(dūn huáng)古乐

在丝绸之路上,有一个地方叫敦煌。那里有一千多年前的壁(bì)画。敦煌壁画很美,有仙女跳舞,有乐队弹奏(zòu)……有人研究,壁画里出现过54种乐器:琴、笛(dí)、琵琶(pí pa)、鼓(gǔ)等。这些乐器,许多都失传了。1900年,敦煌发现了"藏(cáng)经洞"。洞里不仅有5万件古代书画文本,还发现了唐、五代时期的手抄乐谱(pǔ),后来被叫作"敦煌乐谱"。

这些乐谱太宝贵了,是1,700年前的音乐。专家们把壁画上的乐器复制(zhì)出来,配(pèi)上敦煌乐谱,于是,人们又听到了来自唐朝的音乐,不是静止的图画,而是那个时代的声音。

敦煌壁画 "敦煌乐舞"

敦煌壁画

**资料**

认识一下中国古代民间乐器：

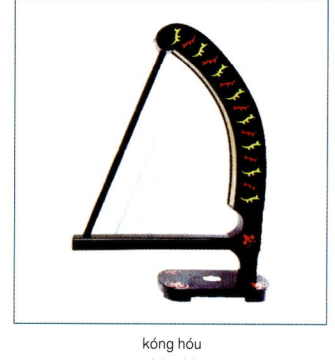

箜篌
kóng hóu

琵琶

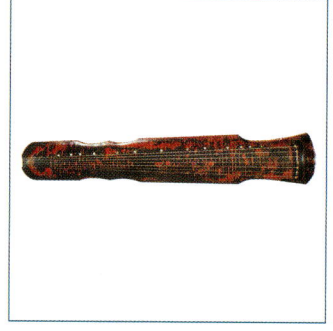

琴

English Translation

# High Mountains and Flowing Water

There is a famous piece of music in China that is called "High Mountains and Flowing Water". When listening to it, you feel like you are in-between heaven and earth, in a landscape of mountains and water, that you merge with the world around you, that heaven and man become one. There is an old story about this music that has been passed on for two-thousand years.

It is said that in the Warring States period, there was a masterful zither player of the State of Chu called Yu Boya, whose art was unrivalled. One evening, as the moon was clear and a clean wind blew, Boya played his zither on a boat. The music rose and flew between the water and the sky. He played and played until suddenly a string broke. Boya thought to himself: "Could somebody be listening?" There was a saying that if somebody who understands music as well as the feelings of the player is listening, the strings of a zither might break. Boya looked around and indeed saw a woodcutter who was listening. The man was wearing a straw hat and carrying an axe, and there was a bundle of brushwood at his feet. His name was Zhong Ziqi. Boya did not expect anyone out in the wilderness would really understand his music, so he thought of testing Zhong Ziqi. He played the tune "High mountains". As soon as he had finished, Zhong Ziqi called out: "Bravo! The lofty height of Mount Tai!" Boya then played the tune "Flowing Waters", the music flowing out between his fingers like the running river. Zhong Ziqi called out again: "Bravo! Brimming and flowing as the river!" As Boya realized that Zhong Ziqi understood his music as nobody else, he was deeply moved and regretted that they had not met earlier. The two men became good friends and promised to meet again on the Moon Festival in the following year.

Boya came back to the same spot in the next year, but was told that Zhong Ziqi was no longer among the living. Great tears flowed out of Boya's eyes. He took his zither to Zhong Ziqi's grave and played and sang to mourn for him. Then he smashed his beloved zither on the gravestone and it broke in two. From that day, Boya never played again because he had lost the person who fully appreciated his playing.

Later on, "High mountains and flowing waters" became a metaphor for "deep mutual understanding".

# High Mountains and Flowing Water

"High mountains and flowing water" is an ancient piece of zither music, a jewel of Chinese music. It's beauty lies in the friendship between Yu Boya, the grand master of the zither, and Zhong Ziqi, who understood this music as nobody else. It witnessed their friendship lasted beyond the grave and symbolized the rarity of achieving real mutual understanding. The piece embodies clarity and loftiness, power of mind and imagination. If you have the opportunity of hearing it when you visit China, don't miss the chance!

# Ancient Music in Dunhuang Murals

Dunhuang is a site on the Silk Road. There are beautiful murals that are over 1000 years old. They show immortal fairies dancing, and musicians playing. Researchers have identified 54 different instruments in the murals, including the zither, the flute, the pipa, drums, and many others. Many of these instruments no longer exist. In 1900, the library Cave were discovered at Dunhuang. In this cave, there are not only 50,000 old manuscripts, but also music scores from the Tang Dynasty and the Five Dynasties. These scores are known as the "Dunhuang scores". They are unique, recording music that was played 1700 years ago. Specialists have reconstructed the instruments shown in the murals and recreated the music from the scores. Thus, we can now not only see the paintings that show the music of the Tang period, but also listen to it.

# 第九课

## 七步诗

曹丕(pī)和曹植都是曹操的儿子。

曹植很聪明，诗歌文章写得又多又好。大家都很佩服曹植，称他是文学家。曹操也很喜欢他，只有曹丕忌妒他。

曹操死后，曹丕做了皇帝。有一天曹植来见哥哥。曹丕没好气地说："我和你虽然是兄弟，但从礼节上来说，是君臣。以后，可不许你仗着自己的才学，不讲君臣的礼节啊！"

薛智广　画

曹植低着头，小心地回答："是。"曹丕又说："父亲在世的时候，你常常拿诗歌文章在别人面前夸耀。那些诗文是不是请别人写的？"曹植说："我从来没有请人帮忙，都是自己写的。"

曹丕板着脸说："好！现在我叫你作一首诗。你走七步，七步走完了，就必须把诗作出来。要不然，就治你的罪。"曹植知道曹丕想害他，说："请出个题目。"曹丕没想到他答应得那么快，心想：好，我就出个难的，看你怎样作！他对曹植说："我和你是兄弟，就用'兄弟'做题目。可是，诗里面不许带有'兄弟'这两个字。"

曹植回答了一声："是！"就走起步来。走一步，念一句，七步还没走完，诗就作出来了：

煮豆燃豆萁（qí），

豆在釜中泣：

本是同根生，

相煎何太急？

这首诗的意思是：

煮豆子烧的是豆秸（jiē）呀，

豆子在锅里伤心地哭泣：

我们本是同一个根上长出来的啊，

你为什么这样着急煮我？

这首诗里，曹植把自己比作豆子，等于说："我们本来是亲兄弟啊！你为什么要害我呢？"

曹丕听完曹植的诗，脸红了，虽然心里不高兴，但是他不能治曹植的罪。

## 生词

| | | | |
|---|---|---|---|
| jì dù 忌妒 | envy | zhì zuì 治罪 | punish sb. for his crime |
| lǐ jié 礼节 | etiquette | tí mù 题目 | topic, subject |
| jūn 君 | monarch | niàn 念 | read |
| zhàng 仗 | depend on | rán 燃 | burn |
| kuā yào 夸耀 | ostentate | fǔ 釜 | pot |
| bǎn zhe liǎn 板着脸 | keep a straight face | jiān 煎 | simmer in water |
| bì xū 必须 | must, have to | kū qì 哭泣 | cry |

## 听写

忌妒　礼节　夸耀　板着脸　治罪　题目　念　必须　燃　煎　哭泣

中国古代故事

## 比一比

前 $\begin{cases} 前面 \\ 前后 \end{cases}$ 　　射 $\begin{cases} 射箭 \\ 神箭手 \end{cases}$ 　　煎 $\begin{cases} 煎鸡蛋 \\ 煎牛排 \end{cases}$

题 $\begin{cases} 题目 \\ 问题 \end{cases}$ 　　礼 $\begin{cases} 礼貌 \\ 礼节 \end{cases}$

## 词语运用

**必须**

① 医生对病人说："这个药必须饭后吃。"

② 看电影必须买票入场。

③ 打球之前，必须先活动活动身体。

**夸耀**

① 齐威王在田忌面前夸耀自己的马。

② 姐姐学习好，常常帮我，但从不夸耀自己。

## 词语解释

忌妒——因为别人比自己好而恨(hèn)别人。

治罪——定罪名并处罚。

### 书信写法

书信：格式分为、称呼、问候(hū)、正文、祝福语、签(qiān)名、日期

## 可概括为三大部分：

1．前文（开头）：称呼，问候

2．正文（信的主要部分）

3．后文（结尾）：祝福语，签名，日期

正文：叙述清楚

祝福语：此致(zhì)、敬礼、祝（另起一行低两格）

写信人签名：右下方，日期

信封(fēng)的写法（横信封）　　邮政编码(mǎ)

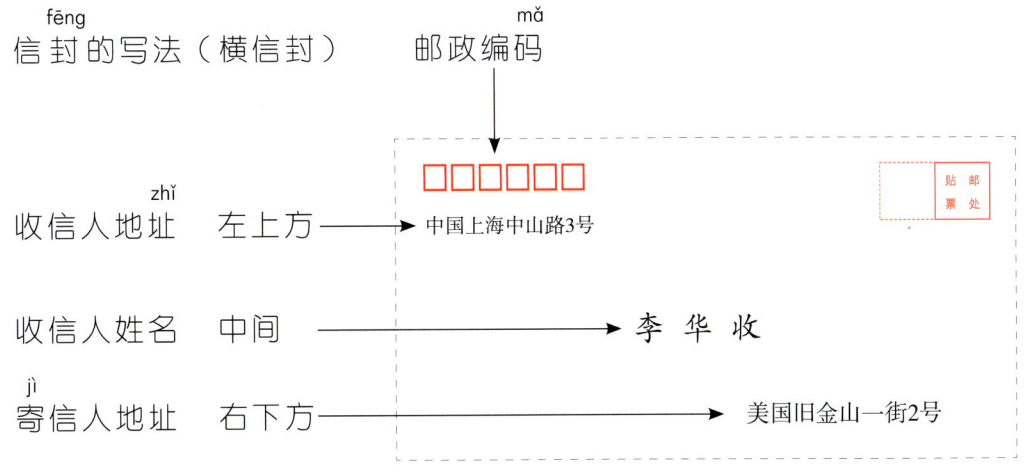

收信人地址(zhǐ)　左上方 —→ 中国上海中山路3号

收信人姓名　中间 —————————→ 李 华 收

寄(jì)信人地址　右下方 ————————→ 美国旧金山一街2号

## 中国古代故事

**范文**

# 给古人写一封信

华佗先生：

  您好！

  我的名字叫牛书衡(héng)。我生活在2010年，是美国的一个小学生。我在中文课上学到一个关于您的故事《三试华佗》。我学到，您是一个很著名的医生，您还发明了麻醉药！我很敬佩您。我听说您在给曹操看病，您可要小心。您要是离开曹操的话，他一定会把您抓起来，再把您杀死。

  我还要送给您一件礼物，是一个听诊器(zhěn)。我要是有更多的钱，就会给您买一个X光机，您就能看见人的骨头长什么样子了。您那个时候当医生，用什么工具？什么药？希望收到您的回信！

  祝您身体健康，工作顺利！

牛书衡

2010年 5月6日

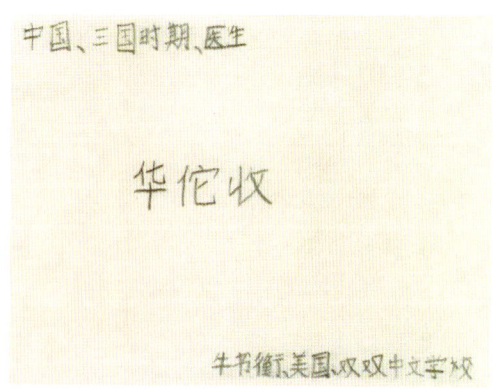

76

English Translation

# The Seven Paces Poem

Cao Pi and Cao Zhi were Cao Cao's sons. Cao Zhi was very intelligent and wrote a lot of good poetry and prose. Everyone admired Cao Zhi and called him a great author. Cao Cao also liked him, but Cao Pi was jealous.

After Cao Cao's death, Cao Pi became the emperor. One day, Cao Zhi came to see his brother. Cao Pi said bad-temperedly: "We are brothers, but in terms of etiquette we are ruler and subject. From now on, I forbid you to brag about your literary talent because this is bad manners between ruler and subject!"

Cao Zhi bowed his head and earnestly answered: "I obey." Then Cao Pi went on: "When father was alive, you often flaunted your poems and your essays in front of others. Did you have help from others?" Cao Zhi answered: "I never had any help, I wrote everything myself."

Cao Pi said grimly: "Fair enough! Now I order you to compose a poem. You will walk seven paces and by the end of the seventh pace you have to have the poem finished. If not, I will have you punished." Cao Zhi realized that Cao Pi wanted him dead and said: "Please set a topic." Cao Pi had not expected his brother to accept so quickly, and thought: "Well, I will give you a difficult topic and see how you handle it!" He said: "You and I are brothers, so let '兄弟 Brothers' be the topic. But you may not use the two characters in the poem."

Cao Zhi replied: "I obey." He began walking and with every step pronounced a line, finishing before he had walked the seven paces:

煮豆燃豆萁，

豆在釜中泣：

本是同根生，

相煎何太急？

Burning the beanstraw to cook beans,

The beans weep in the cauldron:

We grew from the same root.

Why would we burn each other?

In the poem, Cao Zhi compared himself to the beans. He was in fact saying: "We are brothers, why would you want to harm me?" As Cao Zhi finished his poem, Cao Pi was red in the face. Although he was angry, he could not punish Cao Zhi.

# 第十课

## 完璧归赵

战国时期，秦国很强，常常进攻别的国家。

有一回，赵王得了一块珍贵的宝玉——和氏璧。秦王知道后，写信给赵王，愿拿十五座城来换这块宝玉。

赵王看到信，非常着急，马上找大臣们商量。大家都说秦王不过是想把宝玉骗到手，不能上当；可是不答应，又怕他派兵进攻。

正在为难的时候，有人说蔺(lìn)相如勇敢、机智，也许有办法。赵王把蔺相如找来，问他怎么办。蔺相如想了一会儿说："我愿意带着宝玉去秦国，如果秦王不交城，我一定把玉带回来。这样，秦国就没有出兵的理由了。"

蔺相如来到秦国，将宝玉献给秦王。秦王捧着宝玉，一边看一边连连说好，就是不提交城换璧的事。蔺相如看出秦王并无真心，就上前一步说："大王，这块宝玉有点儿小毛病，让我指给您看。"秦王听他这么说，就把宝玉交给了他。蔺相如接过宝玉，后退了几步说："我看您并不想交出十五座城，所以把宝玉拿了回来。您要是逼我,我的脑袋和宝玉就一块儿撞碎在柱子上!"说着,举起宝玉就要往柱子上撞。秦王怕宝玉碎了,连忙把他劝住,说一切都好商量,还叫人拿出地图,把要给赵国的十五座城指给他看。蔺相如又说:"和氏璧是无价之宝,必须举行一个隆重的典礼,我才交出来。"秦王只好和他约定了举行典礼的日期。

蔺相如离开秦王后,马上叫手下人带着宝玉,偷偷回赵国去了。到了典礼那天,蔺相如见了秦王,大大方方地说:"宝玉已送回赵国了,请先交十五座城,我马上将和氏璧送来。不然,您杀了我也没有用。"秦王没有办法,只得客客气气地送蔺相如回国。

蔺相如完璧归赵立了功,赵王封他做上大夫。

## 中国古代故事

汉画像石 "完璧归赵"

## 生词

| | | | |
|---|---|---|---|
| 完璧归赵 wán bì guī zhào | return the jade intact to Zhao State | 举行 jǔ xíng | hold |
| 氏 shì | surnames | 隆重 lóng zhòng | grand |
| 上当 shàng dàng | be fooled | 典礼 diǎn lǐ | ceremony |
| 进攻 jìn gōng | attack | 约(定) yuē dìng | appoint; agree on |
| 机智 jī zhì | wit | 大方 dà fang | generous |
| 献 xiàn | dedicated to | 客气 kè qi | polite |
| 捧 pěng | hold | 封 fēng | seal |
| 逼 bī | force | | |

## 听写

完璧归赵　氏　进攻　机智　捧着　逼　举行　客气　封　*隆重　典礼　约定

## 比一比

封 { 信封 / 封官 }　　举 { 举起 / 举行 }

典 { 典礼 / 字典 }　　礼 { 礼貌 / 敬礼 }

## 反义词

大方——小气　　机智——愚笨

## 多音字

当 dāng　当然

当 dàng　上当

中国古代故事

## 字词运用

举行

① 明天学校举行全校篮球比赛。

② 每年十月,这里都举行华人运动会。

③ 星期三下午,班里举行诗歌表演。

约

① 我和小丽约好明天一起去爬山。

② 我和医生约好明天上午看病。

## 字词解释

完璧归赵——比喻把东西完好地归还物主。

无价之宝——无法估价的宝贝,指极珍贵的东西。

## 阅读

### 荆轲(jīng kē)刺秦王

战国时期,燕(yān)太子丹派荆轲带着燕地图和樊於期(fán wū)首级,前往秦国刺杀秦王。燕太子丹穿着白衣在易水边为荆轲送行,大家留着眼泪。荆轲唱到"风萧萧(xiāo xī)兮易水寒,壮士一去兮不复还(huán)",之后上车而去,再没有回头。

荆轲到秦国,秦王在咸阳宫见他。荆轲拿地图给秦王看,图慢慢展开,一把匕(bǐ)首露出!荆轲左手抓住秦王的衣袖,右手拿起匕首向秦王刺去。秦王使劲挣(zhēng)断袖子就跑,荆轲手拿匕(bǐ)首紧追。秦王围着柱子跑。秦王有剑,但剑太长拔不出。群臣吓呆了,他们身上都没有武器,台下武士没有秦王命令也不能上来。这时有人大喊:"大王,把剑推到背后,推到背后!"秦王拔出宝剑,

汉画像石　荆轲刺秦王

砍伤了荆轲的腿。荆轲倒在地上,他用力将匕首扔向秦王。秦王闪过,匕首扎在柱子上。秦王又向荆轲砍(kǎn)了几剑,荆轲身受多处剑伤,知已失败,苦笑着说:"我没有早下手,本来是想先逼你退还燕国的土地。"卫士上前,荆轲死。

荆轲告别太子丹

### 资料

荆轲(?—前227),战国末期卫国人,著名刺客。受燕太子丹之托刺秦王嬴(yíng)政,失败被杀。《荆轲刺秦王》出自《战国策·燕策三》,在司马迁《史记》中也有记录。

# The Jade Disc and Its Intact Return to Zhao

In the Warring States period, the State of Qin was very powerful, and often waged war on other states.

Once, the King of Zhao obtained a most precious piece of jade, He's Jade Disc. When the King of Qin heard of this, he wrote a letter to the King of Zhao, saying that he would exchange the disc against fifteen cities.

When the King of Zhao received this letter, he was terribly worried and immediately consulted with his ministers. They all agreed that the King of Qin was planning to get hold of the jade and that they must not fall for his ruse. Then again, Zhao could hardly not accept the offer without risking an invasion.

Just as nobody knew a way out, somebody mentioned Lin Xiangru, who was brave and smart, and might be able to save the day. The King of Zhao sent for Lin Xiangru and asked his advice. Lin Xiangru considered the matter and said: "I am willing to take the jade disc to the Qin, and if the King of Qin does not hand over the cities, I promise to bring it back. Thus, Qin would have no reason for war."

Lin Xiangru travelled to Qin and presented the jade disc to the King of Qin. He received it, held it in both hands and admired it, yet never mentioned the cities he would cede in return. Aware of the king's treacherous intent, Lin Xiangru said: "Great King, there is a slight blemish in the jade, let me show it to you." Unsuspectingly, the king handed Lin Xiangru the jade back. Once he had the jade, Lin Xiangru took several steps backward: "I see that you have no intention of handing over the fifteen cities, that is why I took the jade back. If you try to threaten me, I will break my head and the disc against this pillar!" With this, he lifted the jade above his head, ready to strike the pillar. The King of Qin, afraid that Lin Xiangru would break the disc, immediately offered negotiations. He even got somebody to fetch a map and showed him the fifteen cities that were to be ceded to Zhao. At long last Lin Xiangru said: "The He's Jade Disc is a priceless treasure, only after a solemn ceremony can I hand it over." The King of Qin had no choice but to set a day for the ceremony.

Once Lin Xiangru had left the King, he had one of his men take the disc secretly back to Zhao. On the day of the ceremony, Lin Xiangru came to the presence of the King of Qin and said unblinkingly: "I have sent the jade back to Zhao. Once you have handed over the fifteen cities, I will immediately send the jade disc of the He clan to you. Otherwise, killing me would be of little use." The King of Qin again had no choice but to politely escort Lin Xiangru back to Zhao.

For this meritorious deed, the King of Zhao made Lin Xiangru grand counsellor.

# Jing Ke's Attempted Assassination of the King of Qin

In the Warring States period, Crown Prince Dan of Yan sent Jing Ke with a map of Yan and the severed head of Fan Wuqi to assassinate the King of Qin. Crown Prince Dan dressed in white when he parted with Jing Ke at the banks of the Yishui, and all present shed tears. Jing Ke sang "Rustling wind – oh-and the cold waters of the Yishui, a strong man sets out – oh – never to return." Then turned his carriage and left without ever turning back.

When Jing Ke reached Qin, the King of Qin received him in audience. Jing Ke took out the map to show it to the king, and as he unfolded it slowly, a dagger dropped out. Jing Ke grabbed the king's sleeve with his left hand and the dagger with his right to stab the king, but the king managed to pull free and fled. Jing Ke ran after him with the dagger.

The King of Qin ran around the pillars. He had a sword, but it was too long to draw. The ministers were immobilized with fright, and none of them had a weapon on them. The guards below the palace platform were not permitted to come up without the king's orders. At that moment, somebody shouted: "Great King, push the sword back, push it back!" The king managed to draw the sword and wounded Jing Ke in the leg. Jing Ke fell down, but threw his dagger at the king for the last attempt. The king dodged it and the dagger stuck in a pillar. Now the King of Qin attacked him with his sword. Bleeding from several wounds, Jing Ke knew he had failed and said with a bitter smile: "I did no strike earlier because I wanted to force you to return the lands of Yan first..." The guards came, and Jing Ke died.

Jing Ke (? – 227 BC) lived in the late Warring States period. He was from the State of Wei. Crown Prince Dan of Yan sent him to assassinate King Yingzheng of Qin, but he failed and lost his life. The story is recorded in the *Annals of the Warring States* and in Sima Qian's *Shiji*.

# 生字表(简)

1. 柱(zhù) 议(yì) 杆(gǎn) 秤(chèng) 或(huò) 者(zhě) 宰(zǎi) 切(qiē) 赶(gǎn)
2. 忌(jì) 赛(sài) 输(shū) 垂(chuí) 丧(sàng) 败(bài) 锣(luó) 第(dì) 赢(yíng) 顺(shùn) 序(xù)
3. 寄(jì) 杀(shā) 毒(dú) 府(fǔ) 巫(wū) 胆(dǎn) 剑(jiàn) 猎(liè) 吞(tūn) 斗(dòu) 举(jǔ) 砍(kǎn) 勇(yǒng)
4. 矮(ǎi) 旁(páng) 访(fǎng) 接(jiē) 袖(xiù) 既(jì) 规(guī) 矩(jǔ) 犯(fàn) 罪(zuì) 盗(dào) 橘(jú)
5. 豹(bào) 魏(wèi) 娶(qǔ) 淹(yān) 绅(shēn) 硬(yìng) 选(xuǎn) 席(xí) 催(cuī) 跪(guì) 饶(ráo) 渠(qú)
6. 韩(hán) 灭(miè) 懂(dǒng) 貌(mào) 拾(shí) 恭(gōng) 耐(nài) 歉(qiàn) 推(tuī)
7. 醉(zuì) 志(zhì) 诚(chéng) 佩(pèi) 众(zhòng) 默(mò) 考(kǎo) 涯(yá)
8. 若(ruò) 超(chāo) 弹(tán) 悠(yōu) 扬(yáng) 飘(piāo) 弦(xián) 捆(kǔn) 柴(chái) 斧(fǔ) 巍(wēi) 恨(hèn) 欣(xīn)
   赏(shǎng) 妙(miào)
9. 忌(jì) 妒(dù) 君(jūn) 耀(yào) 必(bì) 须(xū) 罪(zuì) 题(tí) 燃(rán) 釜(fǔ) 煎(jiān) 泣(qì)
10. 璧(bì) 氏(shì) 攻(gōng) 献(xiàn) 捧(pěng) 逼(bī) 举(jǔ) 隆(lóng) 封(fēng)

共计110个生字,累计1389个生字

# 生字表（繁）

1. 柱(zhù) 議(yì) 杆(gǎn) 秤(chèng) 或(huò) 者(zhě) 宰(zǎi) 切(qiē) 趕(gǎn)
2. 忌(jì) 賽(sài) 輸(shū) 垂(chuí) 喪(sàng) 敗(bài) 鑼(luó) 第(dì) 贏(yíng) 順(shùn) 序(xù)
3. 寄(jì) 殺(shā) 毒(dú) 府(fǔ) 巫(wū) 膽(dǎn) 劍(jiàn) 獵(liè) 吞(tūn) 鬥(dòu) 舉(jǔ) 砍(kǎn) 勇(yǒng)
4. 矮(ǎi) 旁(páng) 訪(fǎng) 接(jiē) 袖(xiù) 既(jì) 規(guī) 矩(jǔ) 犯(fàn) 罪(zuì) 盜(dào) 橘(jú)
5. 豹(bào) 魏(wèi) 娶(qǔ) 淹(yān) 紳(shēn) 硬(yìng) 選(xuǎn) 席(xí) 催(cuī) 跪(guì) 饒(ráo) 渠(qú)
6. 韓(hán) 滅(miè) 懂(dǒng) 貌(mào) 拾(shí) 恭(gōng) 耐(nài) 歉(qiàn) 推(tuī)
7. 醉(zuì) 志(zhì) 誠(chéng) 佩(pèi) 眾(zhòng) 默(mò) 考(kǎo) 涯(yá)
8. 若(ruò) 超(chāo) 彈(tán) 悠(yōu) 揚(yáng) 飄(piāo) 弦(xián) 捆(kǔn) 柴(chái) 斧(fǔ) 巍(wēi) 恨(hèn) 欣(xīn) 賞(shǎng) 妙(miào)
9. 忌(jì) 妒(dù) 君(jūn) 耀(yào) 必(bì) 須(xū) 罪(zuì) 題(tí) 燃(rán) 釜(fǔ) 煎(jiān) 泣(qì)
10. 璧(bì) 氏(shì) 攻(gōng) 獻(xiàn) 捧(pěng) 逼(bī) 舉(jǔ) 隆(lóng) 封(fēng)

共計110個生字，纍計1389個生字

# 生词表（简）

1. 称(chēng) 末期(mò qī) 官员(guān yuán) 柱(zhù) 到底(dào dǐ) 议论(yì lùn) 杆秤(gǎn chèng) 或者(huòzhě) 宰(zǎi) 切(qiē) 难道(nándào) 连忙(liánmáng) 赶(gǎn) 沿着(yánzhe)

2. 忌(jì) 赛(sài) 大将(dà jiàng) 各自(gè zì) 等级(děng jí) 输(shū) 垂头丧气(chuí tóu sàng qì) 失败(shī bài) 锣(luó) 第一场(dì yī chǎng) 赢(yíng) 调换(diào huàn) 顺序(shùn xù) 转败为胜(zhuǎn bài wéi shèng)

3. 寄(jì) 杀(shā) 毒(dú) 官府(guān fǔ) 反倒(fǎn dào) 巫婆(wū pó) 胆大(dǎn dà) 除害(chú hài) 剑(jiàn) 猎(liè) 丈(zhàng) 吞(tūn) 斗(dòu) 举(jǔ) 砍(kǎn) 勇敢(yǒng gǎn)

4. 出使(chū shǐ) 矮小(ǎi xiǎo) 旁边(páng biān) 访问(fǎng wèn) 迎接(yíng jiē) 袖子(xiù zi) 既然(jì rán) 规矩(guī ju) 犯人(fàn rén) 犯罪(fàn zuì) 强盗(qiáng dào) 橘子(jú zi) 安居乐业(ān jū lè yè) 取笑(qǔ xiào)

5. 豹(bào) 魏(wèi) 管理(guǎn lǐ) 娶亲(qǔ qīn) 淹(yān) 官绅(guān shēn) 硬(yìng) 新娘(xīn niáng) 选(xuǎn) 打扮(dǎ ban) 草席(cǎo xí) 催(cuī) 求饶(qiú ráo) 水渠(shuǐ qú)

6. 拜师(bài shī) 功臣(gōng chén) 韩(hán) 灭(miè) 刺杀(cì shā) 吃惊(chī jīng) 懂(dǒng) 礼貌(lǐ mào) 拾(shí) 恭敬(gōng jìng) 耐心(nài xīn) 教导(jiào dǎo) 约会(yuē huì) 道歉(dào qiàn) 推翻(tuī fān)

7. 发明(fā míng) 麻醉药(má zuì yào) 痛苦(tòng kǔ) 立志(lì zhì) 精通(jīng tōng) 医术(yī shù) 诚心(chéng xīn) 摸脉(mō mài) 的确(dí què) 佩服(pèi fú) 众(zhòng) 幸好(xìng hǎo) 默写(mò xiě) 考试(kǎo shì) 告别(gào bié) 生涯(shēng yá)

中国古代故事

8. 若　琴艺　高超　弹琴　悠扬　飘　琴弦　一捆柴　斧头
   巍巍　如此　知音　相见恨晚　欣赏　美妙

9. 忌妒　礼节　君　仗　夸耀　板着脸　必须　治罪　题目
   念　燃　釜　煎　哭泣

10. 完璧归赵　氏　上当　进攻　机智　献　捧　逼
    举行　隆重　典礼　约（定）　大方　客气　封

共计148个生词

# 生词表（繁）

1. 稱 末期 官員 柱 到底 議論 杆秤 或者 宰 切 難道 連忙 趕 沿著

2. 忌 賽 大將 各自 等級 輸 垂頭喪氣 失敗 鑼 第一場 贏 調換 順序 轉敗爲勝

3. 寄 殺 毒 官府 反倒 巫婆 膽大 除害 劍 獵 丈 吞 鬥 舉 砍 勇敢

4. 出使 矮小 旁邊 訪問 迎接 袖子 既然 規矩 犯人 犯罪 強盜 橘子 安居樂業 取笑

5. 豹 魏 管理 娶親 淹 官紳 硬 新娘 選 打扮 草席 催 求饒 水渠

6. 拜師 功臣 韓 滅 刺殺 吃驚 懂 禮貌 拾 恭敬 耐心 教導 約會 道歉 推翻

7. 發明 麻醉藥 痛苦 立志 精通 醫術 誠心 摸脈 的確 佩服 衆 幸好 默寫 考試 告別 生涯

中国古代故事

8. 若 琴藝 高超 彈琴 悠揚 飄 琴弦 一捆柴 斧頭
   巍巍 如此 知音 相見恨晚 欣賞 美妙

9. 忌妒 禮節 君 仗 誇耀 板著臉 必須 治罪 題目
   念 燃 釜 煎 哭泣

10. 完璧歸趙 氏 上當 進攻 機智 獻 捧 逼
    舉行 隆重 典禮 約（定） 大方 客氣 封

共計148個生詞

# 附录

## "新双双中文教材"写作练习（1—8册）

课文正式教授写作内容

| 内容 | 出处 | 建议学习年级 |
| --- | --- | --- |
| 1. 课文缩写 | 第4册《猴子捞月亮》 | 3—4年级 |
| 2. 日记 | 第5册《妈妈教我写日记》 | 4—5年级 |
| 3. 叙事文 | 第5册《参观兵马俑》 | 4—5年级 |
| 4. 看图写故事 | 第6册 成语故事《塞翁失马》 | 5—6年级 |
| 5. 城市介绍 | 第7册 中国地理常识《著名城市》 | 5—6年级 |
| 6. 书信 | 第8册 中国古代故事《七步诗》 | 5—6年级 |

辅助写作练习

| 内容 | 出处 | 建议学习年级 |
| --- | --- | --- |
| 1. 读书笔记 | 亲子阅读，每周家庭读书、写作 | 2—6年级 |
| 2. 观察记录 | 第4册 写《养蚕报告》 | 3—4年级 |
| 3. 创作 | 写简单的故事和想法 | 4年级以上 |

# 新双双中文教材 8
New Chinese Language and Culture Course

## 中国古代故事 Ancient Chinese Stories

练习本 单课

王双双 编著

北京大学出版社
PEKING UNIVERSITY PRESS

# 目　录

第一课　曹冲称象 …………………………………… 1

第三课　李寄杀蛇 …………………………………… 6

第五课　西门豹的故事 ……………………………… 11

第七课　三试华佗 …………………………………… 16

第九课　七步诗 ……………………………………… 21

# 第一课 曹冲称象

## 一 写生词

| 称 | | | | | |
|---|---|---|---|---|---|
| 柱 | | | | | |
| 杆 | | | | | |
| 秤 | | | | | |
| 宰 | | | | | |
| 切 | | | | | |
| 赶 | | | | | |

| 末 | 期 | | | | |
|---|---|---|---|---|---|
| 官 | 员 | | | | |
| 到 | 底 | | | | |
| 议 | 论 | | | | |
| 或 | 者 | | | | |
| 难 | 道 | | | | |
| 连 | 忙 | | | | |
| 沿 | 着 | | | | |

## 二 组词

议_____ 官_____ 或_____ 沿_____

## 三 下列汉字是由哪些部分组成的

秤 — 禾 + 平　　　　　　赶 — ☐ + ☐

称 — ☐ + ☐　　　　　　杆 — ☐ + ☐

## 第一课 曹冲称象

### 四 选字组词

官（园 员）　　（主 柱）人　　一杆（称 秤）

花（园 员）　　（主 柱）子　　称一（称 秤）

### 五 你在"辛"字中看出几个字？请写出

| 1 | 2 | 3 | 4 |

（辛｜立／一｜十）

### 六 选词填空

1. 上学别忘了_____作业。（代 带）

2. 外面很冷，出去一定要_____帽子。（戴 袋）

3. 这象_____有多重呢？官员们议论着。（到底 底下）

4. 把大象赶到_____大船上。（一条 一杆）

### 七 选择填空

曹操是一位：

• _____

• _____

• _____

军事家　诗人　政治家　数学家　画家　科学家

## 第一课 曹冲称象

### 八 根据课文判断对错

1. 三国时期有个著名的政治家叫曹操。　　　　　___对___错

2. 这象到底有多重呢？孩子们议论着。　　　　　___对___错

3. 造一杆大秤来称象的主意不错。　　　　　　　___对___错

4. 把大象宰了切成块再称的主意不好。　　　　　___对___错

5. 曹冲只有六岁，但很聪明。　　　　　　　　　___对___错

### 九 造句

难道_____

或者_____

### 十 根据阅读《曹冲》回答问题

1. 仆人吓哭了，意思是仆人_____。

  A. 高高兴兴　　　　B. 非常害怕

2. 曹冲13岁时得病去世了。"去世"意思是_____。

  A. 活着　　　　　　B. 死去

3. 曹冲生活在_____。

  A. 二千多年前　　　B. 一千多年前

# 第一课 曹冲称象

## 十一 认一认

繁体与简体的"汉"字

| 漢 | 漢朝 | 漢族 | 漢人 | 漢字 |

| 汉 | 汉朝 | 汉族 | 汉人 | 汉字 |

a 用繁体写一遍上面的四个词

| 漢 | □ | □ | □ | □ |

b 翻开字典找一找有关"汉"字组成的词

1. ___汉语___      2. _____      3. _____

4. _____      5. _____      6. _____

### 第一课 曹冲称象

**十二 根据阅读《我从汉朝来》选择填空**

　　1. 汉朝建立于_____。（公元前206年　公元206年）

　　2. 汉朝时中国成为_____强盛的帝国。（统一　分裂）

　　3. 汉朝和罗马帝国处在_____时期。（同一　不同）

　　4. 汉朝和罗马帝国都是文明_____的大帝国。（先进　落后）

　　5. 人们称中国字为____。（蒙古字　汉字）

**十三　朗读课文三遍**

## 第三课 李寄杀蛇

一 写生词

| 寄 | | | | | |
|---|---|---|---|---|---|
| 杀 | | | | | |
| 毒 | | | | | |
| 剑 | | | | | |
| 猎 | | | | | |
| 丈 | | | | | |
| 吞 | | | | | |
| 斗 | | | | | |

| 举 | | | | | |
|---|---|---|---|---|---|
| 砍 | | | | | |
| 官 | 府 | | | | |
| 反 | 倒 | | | | |
| 巫 | 婆 | | | | |
| 胆 | 大 | | | | |
| 除 | 害 | | | | |
| 勇 | 敢 | | | | |

二 组词

丈 { 一丈 / 丈夫　　官 { ___　　猎 { ___

握 { ___　　胆 { ___　　害 { ___

三 下列汉字是由哪些部分组成的

胆 — 月 + 旦　　砍 — ☐ + ☐

握 — ☐ + ☐　　婆 — ☐ + ☐

# 第三课
## 李寄杀蛇

四 你在"**胆**"字中看出几个字？请写出来

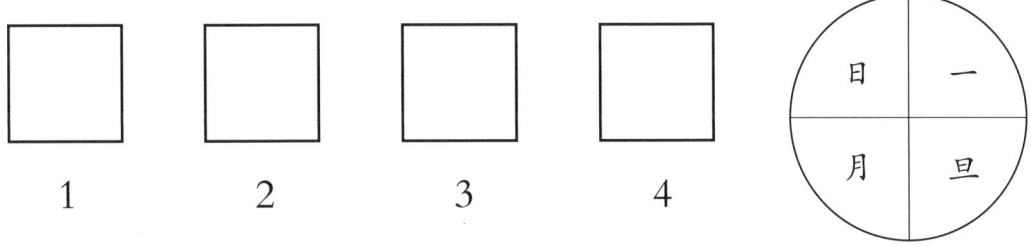

   1        2        3        4

五 先组字，再组词

"才"字进口是 团 ， 团结

"玉"字进口是 □ ， _____

"冬"字进口是 □ ， _____

"元"字进口是 □ ， _____

"大"字进口是 □ ， _____

六 造句

勇敢_____

举起_____

## 第三课 李寄杀蛇

### 七 选择填空

1. 大蛇_____出来伤人。

   A. 常常　　　　B. 长长

2. 有一个女孩儿叫_____，胆大过人。

   A. 李奇　　　　B. 季寄　　　　C. 李寄

3. 蛇吃饭团时，李寄放出_____咬蛇。

   A. 野猪　　　　B. 猎狗

4. 李寄一个箭步跳起，高举青龙剑向蛇背_____去。

   A. 吹　　　　B. 砍　　　　C. 次

5. _____的李寄，杀死了毒蛇，为民除了害。

   A. 聪明勇敢　　　　B. 胆小

### 八 选择填空

曹冲　孙膑　李寄　花木兰

1. _____是曹操的儿子。

2. 古代，一位杀蛇为民除害的女孩叫_____。

3. 田忌赛马时他的朋友_____帮他赢了齐王。

4. _____是古代一位代父亲当兵的勇敢女孩儿。

# 第三课
## 李寄杀蛇

九 看图写话"李寄杀蛇"(至少五句)

提示:蛇多长?眼睛什么样?李寄手里拿着什么?

十 李寄是勇敢的女孩儿,你想对她说什么?请写出来

## 第三课 李寄杀蛇

**十一　写出标点符号**

| 句号 | 逗号 | 叹号 | 冒号 | 引号 |
|------|------|------|------|------|
|      |      |      |      |      |

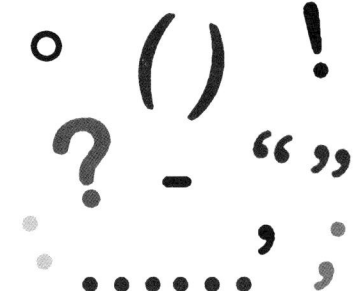

**十二　给下列句子加上标点符号**

1. 野骆驼和大熊猫都是珍稀动物

2. 有个小女孩　她只有十三岁　却胆大过人

3. 曹冲说　我有好办法

4. 田忌说　当然不服气　咱们再赛一次

5. 大象又高又大　身体像一面墙

6. 这时候　姐姐回来了　看见衣服脏了　很不高兴　我赶快对姐姐说对不起　是我的错　我这就去洗

**十三　朗读课文两遍**

## 第五课 西门豹的故事

一 写生词

| 豹 |  |  |  |  |  |
|---|---|---|---|---|---|
| 魏 |  |  |  |  |  |
| 淹 |  |  |  |  |  |
| 硬 |  |  |  |  |  |
| 选 |  |  |  |  |  |
| 催 |  |  |  |  |  |
| 管 | 理 |  |  |  |  |

| 娶 | 亲 |  |  |  |  |
|---|---|---|---|---|---|
| 官 | 绅 |  |  |  |  |
| 新 | 娘 |  |  |  |  |
| 打 | 扮 |  |  |  |  |
| 草 | 席 |  |  |  |  |
| 求 | 饶 |  |  |  |  |
| 水 | 渠 |  |  |  |  |

二 选字组词

（选 先）后　　　（取 娶）亲　　　面（扮 粉）

挑（选 先）　　　（取 娶）书　　　打（扮 粉）

三 给下面的字加拼音，再组词

引_____　_____　　蚓_____　_____

张_____　_____　　*弓_____　_____

引水
张开
蚯蚓

## 第五课 西门豹的故事

### 四 连一连

求饶 —— 请求放过自己

娶亲 —— 指结婚

办喜事 —— 男人娶妻子

催 —— 让人快一点

### 五 照样子在方框中写画出"席"字的演变

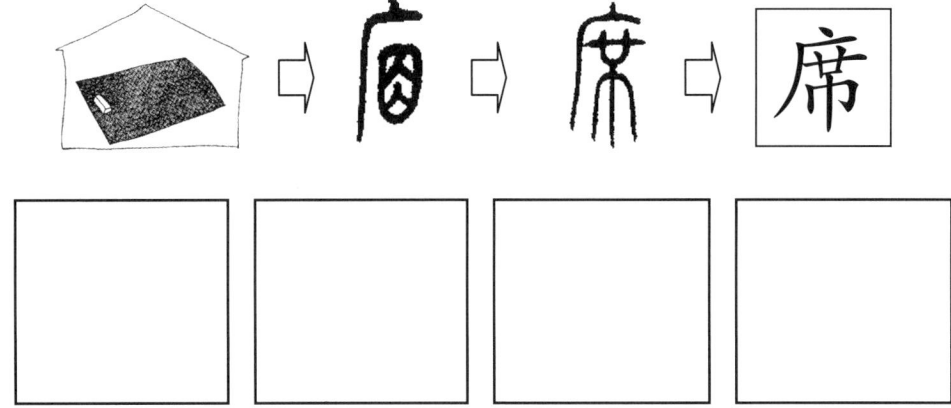

### 六 选词填空

1. 魏王派西门豹去_____邺这个地方。（管理　清理）

2. 哪家有年轻的女孩子，巫婆就到哪家去_____。（选　先）

3. 富绅们个个吓得面如土色，_____求饶。（跪下　危险）

4. 老百姓明白了巫婆和官绅是_____钱害人的。（骗　遍）

5. 西门豹带领老百姓开_____。（水管　水渠）

## 第五课 西门豹的故事

☆ ------------- ☆ ------------- ☆

### 七 根据课文判断对错

1. 西门豹是战国时期人。　　　　　　　　　　___对___错

2. 西门豹看见新娘满脸泪水。　　　　　　　　___对___错

3. 河神娶亲那天,西门豹救了新娘。　　　　　___对___错

4. 西门豹让巫婆去催一催官绅头子。　　　　　___对___错

5. 巫婆、官绅给河神娶亲是为了骗钱。　　　　___对___错

6. 西门豹是个聪明的好官。　　　　　　　　　___对___错

### 八 造句

例：① 每次上课,李老师都打扮得很好看。

②　我催妹妹快点儿做完作业,好去看电影。

打扮_____

催_____

## 第五课 西门豹的故事

**九 填写标点**

| 。 ， ： " " |
|---|

西门豹对巫婆说 不行 这个姑娘不漂亮 河神不会满意的 请你去跟河神说一声 我选个漂亮的 过几天送去 说完 叫卫士抱起巫婆扔进了漳河

**十 比较句子,哪句更生动?在细节描写处画线**

1. 巫婆把新娘领来,西门豹看见一个女孩儿。

   巫婆把新娘领来,西门豹一看,女孩儿满脸泪水。

2. 巫婆在河里沉下去了。

   巫婆在河里扑腾了几下,沉下去了。

3. 那些官绅都吓得跪下求饶。

   那些官绅都吓得面如土色,跪下求饶。

## 第五课 西门豹的故事

十一　给加点的字加拼音

　　1. 树叶顺水漂走。（　　　）

　　2. 姐姐今天打扮得很漂亮。（　　　）

十二　分角色朗读课文两遍或表演课本剧

## 第七课
### 三试华佗

一 写生词

| 众 | | | | | | | 的 | 确 | | | | | |
| 发 | 明 | | | | | | 佩 | 服 | | | | | |
| 痛 | 苦 | | | | | | 幸 | 好 | | | | | |
| 立 | 志 | | | | | | 默 | 写 | | | | | |
| 精 | 通 | | | | | | 考 | 试 | | | | | |
| 医 | 术 | | | | | | 告 | 别 | | | | | |
| 诚 | 心 | | | | | | 生 | 涯 | | | | | |
| 摸 | 脉 | | | | | | 麻 | 醉 | 药 | | | | |

二 组词

幸 { _____  _____ }　　　术 { _____  _____ }

诚 { _____  _____ }　　　别 { _____  _____ }

三 下列汉字是由哪些字组成的

确 — 石 + 角　　　诚 — ☐ + ☐

众 — ☐ + ☐　　　志 — ☐ + ☐

# 第七课 三试华佗

## 四 选字组词

摸（脉　泳）　　（诚　城）心　　（考　烤）试

游（脉　泳）　　（诚　城）市　　（考　烤）肉

## 五 比较"醉"字和"醒"字

但愿长醉不愿醒

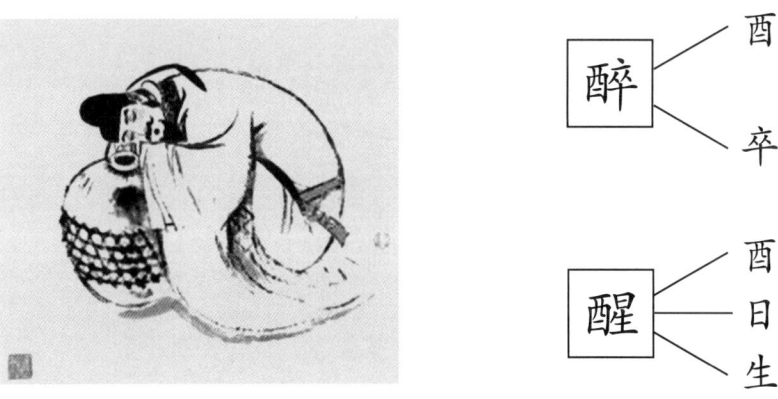

醉 — 酉 / 卒

醒 — 酉 / 日 / 生

提示：人喝醉酒昏睡，有些像死过去一样；第二天酒醒，又正常生活了。

# 第七课
## 三试华佗

六 看图选词填空

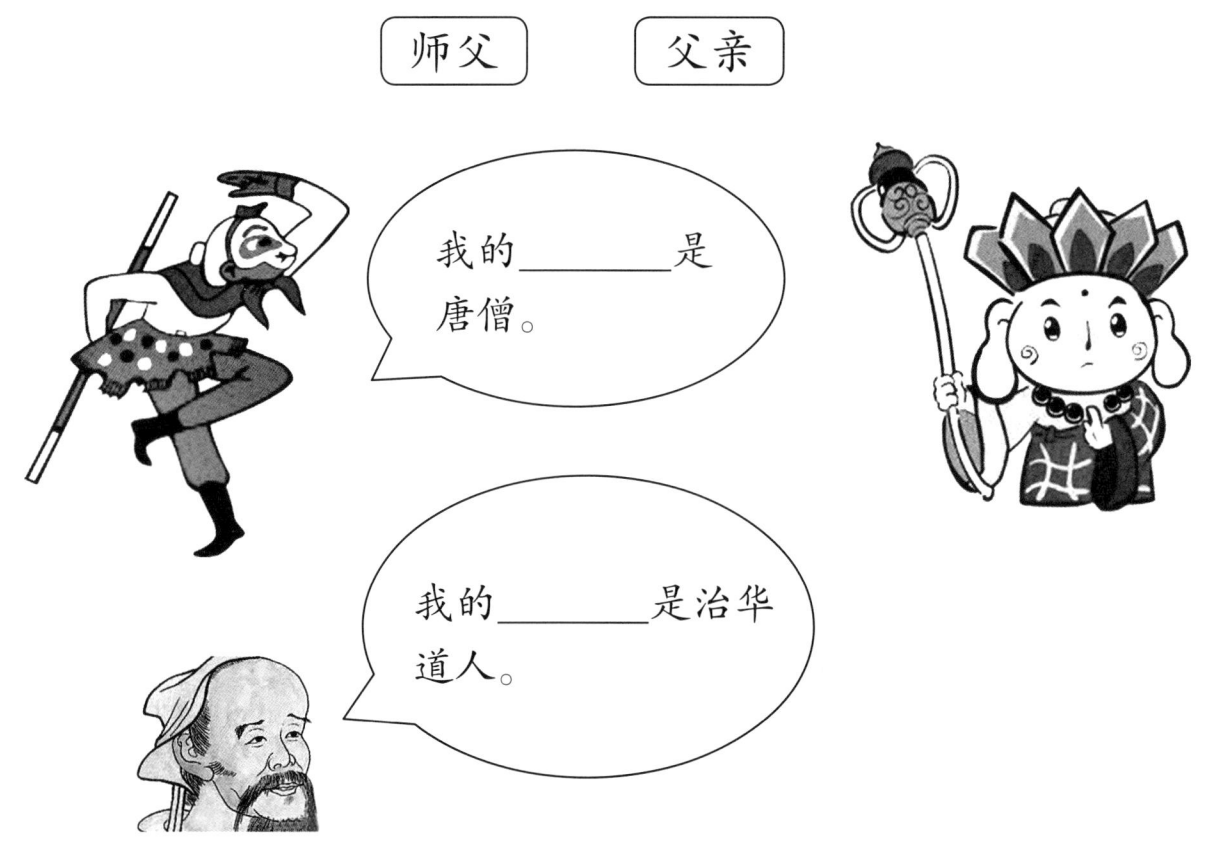

七 选词填空

1. 华佗是_____时期的名医。（三国　春秋）

2. 华佗母亲得病死去后，他立志学医____人。（救　求）

3. 华佗给师父摸了一下____。（脉　永）

4. 幸好华佗可以把医书_____出来。（默写　听写）

5. 华佗告别了师父，开始治病救人的_____。（生涯　生活）

## 第七课 三试华佗

### 八 根据课文判断对错

1. 华佗是三国时期的名医，他发明了麻醉药。　　___对___错

2. 华佗不分白天黑夜地照看病人。　　　　　　　___对___错

3. 师父让华佗快快地读书。　　　　　　　　　　___对___错

4. 华佗可以默写医书。　　　　　　　　　　　　___对___错

5. 华佗的师父叫治华和尚。　　　　　　　　　　___对___错

### 九 师父怎样考华佗，写出三次考试的内容

| 第一次考试内容 | 第二次考试内容 | 第三次考试内容 |
|---|---|---|
| | | |
| | | |
| | | |
| | | |
| | | |
| | | |
| | | |

## 第七课
### 三试华佗

☆ ------------- ☆ ------------- ☆

**十 造句**

的确_____

幸好_____

**十一 根据阅读《华佗和"麻沸散"》选择填空**

1. 华佗精通_____，人们称他为"神医"。

　　A. 歌舞表演　　　　B. 外科手术

2. 一个病人喝醉酒了，病人_____，失去了知觉。

　　A. 烂醉如泥　　　　B. 清清楚楚

3. 华佗发明了中药"_____"，让病人用酒服下。

　　A. 麻沸散　　　　　B. 人参

**十二 给下面带点的字加拼音**

1. 北京烤鸭的确好吃。（　　　）

2. 我的书包太重了。（　　　）

**十三 朗读课文三遍**

## 第九课 七步诗

☆ ———— ☆ ———— ☆

**一 写生词**

| 君 | | | | | |
|---|---|---|---|---|---|
| 仗 | | | | | |
| 念 | | | | | |
| 燃 | | | | | |
| 釜 | | | | | |
| 煎 | | | | | |
| 忌 | 妒 | | | | |

| 礼 | 节 | | | | |
|---|---|---|---|---|---|
| 夸 | 耀 | | | | |
| 必 | 须 | | | | |
| 治 | 罪 | | | | |
| 题 | 目 | | | | |
| 哭 | 泣 | | | | |
| 板 | 着 | 脸 | | | |

**二 组词**

题 { _____    礼 { _____

仗 { _____    煎 { _____

**三 下列汉字是由哪些字组成的**

罪 — 四 + 非          妒 — □ + □

题 — □ + □          燃 — □ + □

21

# 第九课 七步诗

四 抄写曹植的七步诗（竖行）

煮豆燃豆萁
豆在釜中泣
本是同根生
相煎何太急

五 选适当的词填进圈里

釜　豆萁　曹植　燃

## 第九课 七步诗

### 六 选词填空

1. "板着脸"的意思是_____。（不高兴　很快乐）

2. 这次数学考试的_____都很容易。（题目　难题）

3. 小弟弟_____奶奶喜欢他就乱闹。（仗着　打仗）

4. 不同民族的结婚_____都不相同。（礼节　礼貌）

5. 小学生应该讲卫生，有_____。（礼节　礼貌）

### 七 根据课文判断对错

1. 曹植是曹丕的哥哥。　　　　　　　　　　　　___对___错

2. 因为曹植诗文写得好，曹丕嫉妒他。　　　　　___对___错

3. 曹丕让曹植走七步，就得作出一首诗。　　　　___对___错

4. 曹植十步还没走完，诗就作出来了。　　　　　___对___错

5. 曹丕想害曹植，但是没害成。　　　　　　　　___对___错

6. "本是同根生，相煎何太急"意思是：我们是亲

   兄弟，为什么要苦苦相逼。　　　　　　　　　___对___错

### 八 造句

必须_____

## 第九课 七步诗

九 写信（任选一个题目）

- 给朋友或亲人写一封信

- 写一封信给课本中学过的古人，如：曹冲、李寄、晏子、华佗等

先介绍自己，再说你怎么知道他的，为什么想和他做朋友，想送给他什么礼物。

注意：
- 称呼、问候、正文、祝福语、签名、日期
- 信封的写法

信封

## 第九课
### 七步诗

## 第一课　听写

| 1. | 2. | 3. | 4. |
| --- | --- | --- | --- |
| 5. | 6. | 7. | 8. |
| 9. | 10. | 11. | 12. |

## 第三课　听写

| 1. | 2. | 3. | 4. |
| --- | --- | --- | --- |
| 5. | 6. | 7. | 8. |
| 9. | 10. | 11. | 12. |

## 第五课　听写

| 1. | 2. | 3. | 4. |
| --- | --- | --- | --- |
| 5. | 6. | 7. | 8. |
| 9. | 10. | 11. | 12. |

## 第七课　听写

| 1. | 2. | 3. | 4. |
| --- | --- | --- | --- |
| 5. | 6. | 7. | 8. |
| 9. | 10. | 11. | 12. |

# 第九课　听写

| 1. | 2. | 3. | 4. |
|---|---|---|---|
| 5. | 6. | 7. | 8. |
| 9. | 10. | 11. | 12. |

| 1. | 2. | 3. | 4. |
|---|---|---|---|
| 5. | 6. | 7. | 8. |
| 9. | 10. | 11. | 12. |

| 1. | 2. | 3. | 4. |
|---|---|---|---|
| 5. | 6. | 7. | 8. |
| 9. | 10. | 11. | 12. |

| 1. | 2. | 3. | 4. |
|---|---|---|---|
| 5. | 6. | 7. | 8. |
| 9. | 10. | 11. | 12. |

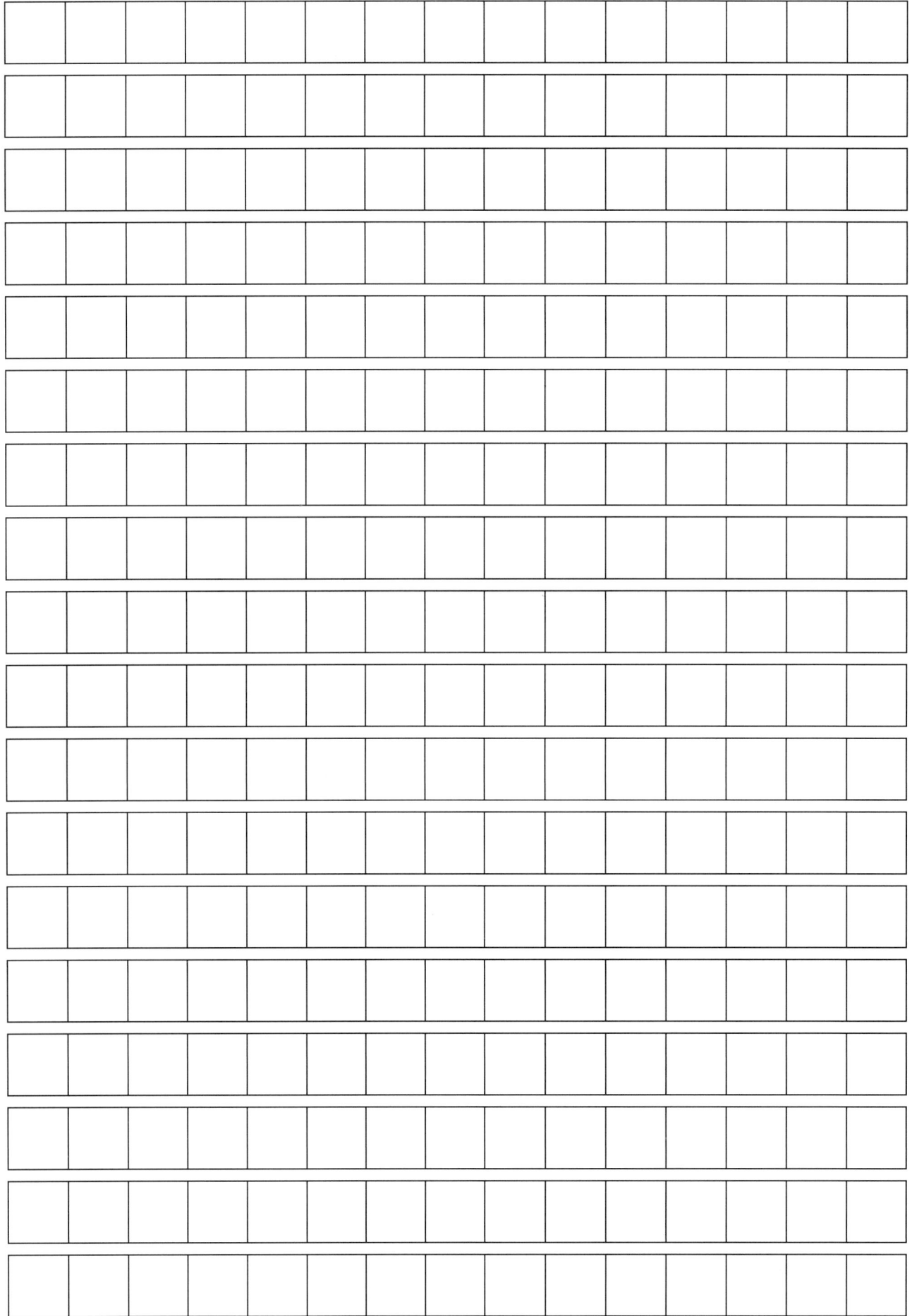

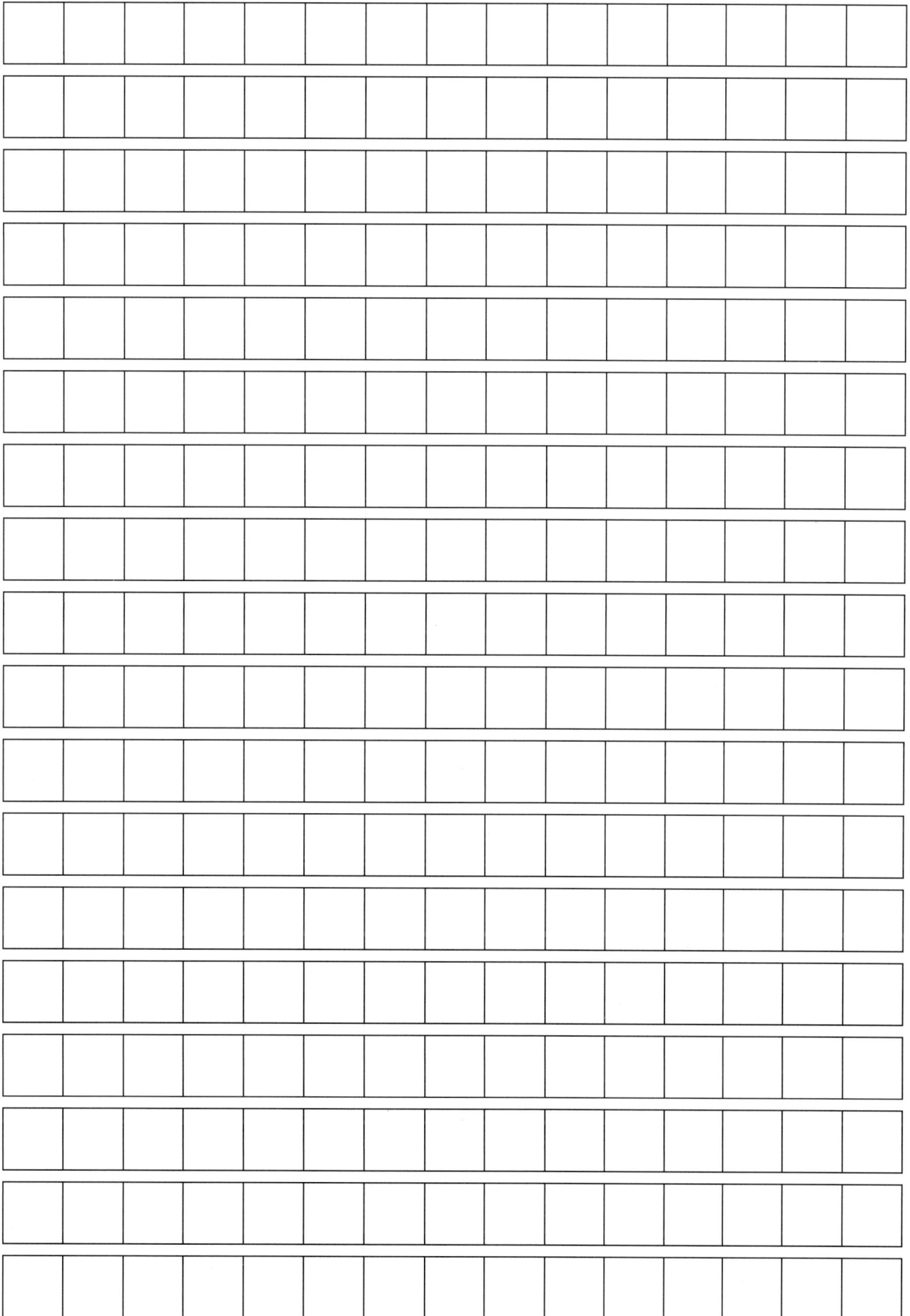

# 新双双中文教材 8
New Chinese Language and Culture Course

## 中国古代故事 Ancient Chinese Stories

练习本 双课

王双双 编著

北京大学出版社
PEKING UNIVERSITY PRESS

# 目　录

第二课　田忌赛马 …………………………………… 1

第四课　晏子使楚 …………………………………… 6

第六课　张良拜师 …………………………………… 11

第八课　高山流水 …………………………………… 15

第十课　完璧归赵 …………………………………… 19

## 第二课 田忌赛马

## 一 写生词

| 忌 | | | | |
|---|---|---|---|---|
| 赛 | | | | |
| 输 | | | | |
| 锣 | | | | |
| 赢 | | | | |
| 大 | 将 | | | |
| 各 | 自 | | | |
| 等 | 级 | | | |

| 失 | 败 | | | |
|---|---|---|---|---|
| 调 | 换 | | | |
| 顺 | 序 | | | |
| 第 | 一 | 场 | | |
| 垂 | 头 | 丧 | 气 | |
| 转 | 败 | 为 | 胜 | |

## 二 找出有相同字的词，写在一组

调换　等级　调皮　大将　年级　将来

{ _____　　{ _____　　{ _____

# 第二课
## 田忌赛马

### 三 你在"赢"字中看出几个字？请写出来

| 1 | 2 | 3 | 4 | 5 |

### 四 看提示把"赢"字中每个字的意思填上

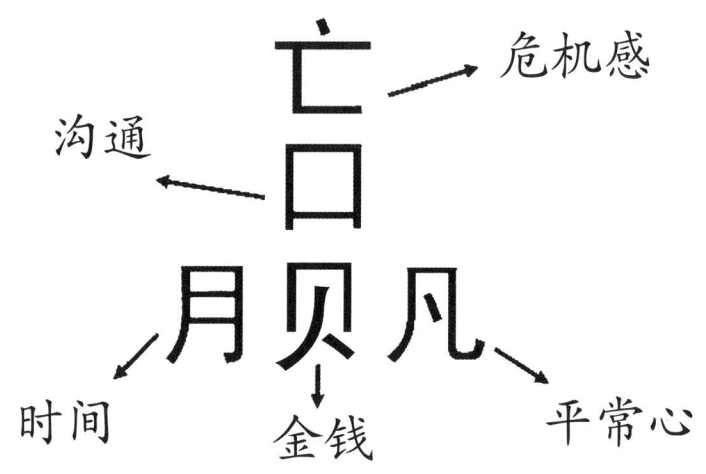

亡＿＿＿＿＿＿＿＿

口＿＿＿＿＿＿＿＿

月＿＿＿＿＿＿＿＿

贝＿＿＿＿＿＿＿＿

凡＿＿＿＿＿＿＿＿

| 提示 |
|---|
| 赢需要努力一段时间 |
| 看到危机就容易赢 |
| 赢得金钱 |
| 会沟通就容易赢 |
| 有平常心就容易赢 |

## 第二课 田忌赛马

五 在方格里照样写一个"输"字（输：原意运输；车字旁）

六 看图连线

得意洋洋

垂头丧气

七 写出反义词

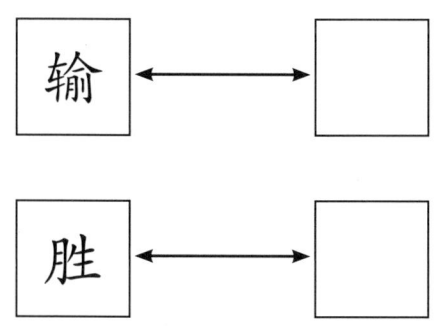

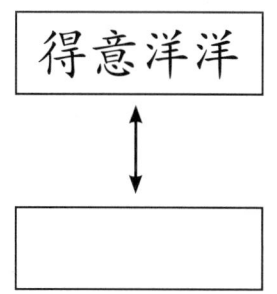

# 第二课
## 田忌赛马

## 八 回答问题

考试的顺序应该是：

1. 把会做的题做完，再想不会的题。

2. 按考题顺序做。

　　回答_____

## 九 选词填空

1. 田忌和齐王_____。（赛篮球　赛马　赛车）

2. 爸爸到银行去换_____。（钱　衣服）

3. 我们在地铁站排队，按_____上车。（顺序　顺路）

4. 田忌是齐国的_____。（将军　将来）

5. 孙膑让田忌_____马出场的顺序。（调皮　调换）

## 十 根据课文判断对错

1. 齐威王和孙膑赛马。　　　　　　　　　　　　____对____错

2. 第一次比赛，田忌三场都赢了。　　　　　　　____对____错

3. 田忌有个好朋友叫孙膑。　　　　　　　　　　____对____错

## 第二课
### 田忌赛马

☆ ------------ ☆ ------------ ☆

4. 齐威王得意洋洋地夸自己的马。　　　　___对___错

5. 做任何事情安排顺序很重要。　　　　　　___对___错

### 十一 写一写

你生活中什么事顺序安排对了，情况就好一些，反之结果就不好。

提示：放学回家，先做完作业，再玩游戏

　　　　体育课，先活动身体，再开始训练

_____

_____

_____

### 十二 阅读作业，选择填空

1. 看汉画像石《力士图》，写出图中有哪些体育活动？

| 游泳 | 拔树 | 斗虎 | 打马球 | 斗牛 | 举鼎 | 背牛 |

有人_____，有人_____，有人_____，有人_____

2. 唐代开放，风行马球，女子也_____。（打马球　篮球）

### 十三 朗读课文三遍

## 第四课 晏子使楚

## 一 写生词

| 出 | 使 |  |  |  |  |
|---|---|---|---|---|---|
| 矮 | 小 |  |  |  |  |
| 旁 | 边 |  |  |  |  |
| 访 | 问 |  |  |  |  |
| 迎 | 接 |  |  |  |  |
| 袖 | 子 |  |  |  |  |
| 既 | 然 |  |  |  |  |

| 规 | 矩 |  |  |  |  |
|---|---|---|---|---|---|
| 犯 | 人 |  |  |  |  |
| 犯 | 罪 |  |  |  |  |
| 强 | 盗 |  |  |  |  |
| 橘 | 子 |  |  |  |  |
| 取 | 笑 |  |  |  |  |
| 安 | 居 | 乐 | 业 |  |  |
|  |  |  |  |  |  |

## 二 组词

旁＿＿＿＿　　袖＿＿＿＿　　盗＿＿＿＿　　访＿＿＿＿

迎＿＿＿＿　　橘＿＿＿＿　　犯＿＿＿＿　　安居＿＿＿＿

## 三 选字组词

（访　方）问　　　强（盗　次）　　　（淮　准）河

（访　方）向　　　两（盗　次）　　　（淮　准）备

## 第四课
## 晏子使楚

四 "没有规矩不成方圆","规""矩"是什么东西？
　请连线

规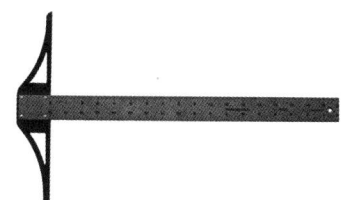

矩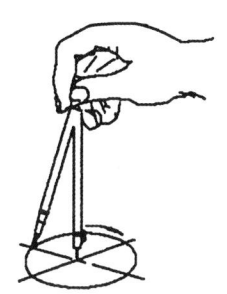

五 选择填空

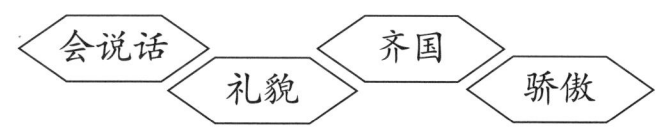

　　晏子是_____的大夫。

　　晏子很_____。

　　楚王太_____了。

　　楚王没有_____。

### 第四课 晏子使楚

## 六 选词填空

1. 晏子身材_____。（高大　矮小）

2. 楚王只好打开城门把_____迎接进去。（晏子　燕子）

3. 楚王说："_____有这么多人，为什么派你来呢？（既然　自然）

4. _____的橘子又大又甜。（淮南　淮北）

## 七 根据课文判断对错

1. 春秋时期，齐王派晏子出使楚国。　　　　　　　___对___错

2. 楚王想为难为难晏子。　　　　　　　　　　　　___对___错

3. 楚王在城门旁开了个五尺高的洞。　　　　　　　___对___错

4. 晏子说："只有访问'狗国'才从狗洞进去。"　　___对___错

5. 晏子比楚王聪明多了。　　　　　　　　　　　　___对___错

## 八 造句

既然_____

访问_____

## 第四课 晏子使楚

## 九 写出标点符号

| 问号 | 分号 | 省略号 | 顿号 |
|------|------|--------|------|
|      |      |        |      |

## 十 填写标点

```
？ 。 ， ： " " 、 ；
```

1. 青蛙问小鸟　你从哪里来呀

2. 昨天　我们全家去长城了

3. 我们买了白菜　苹果　面包和糖

4. 晏子说　我国有个规矩　访问上等的国家　就派上等人去　访问下等的国家　就派下等人　我最不中用　就派到这儿来了

## 十一 给下面这段文字加标点

老黄雀把小虫喂到小黄雀嘴里　那只小黄雀吃得可香了　它问妈妈　这是什么呀　真好吃　老黄雀说　这是卷叶虫　这种虫子很狡猾　它吐出丝　把树叶卷起来　自己躲在里面吃叶肉

## 第四课
### 晏子使楚

十二 写一写为什么橘树种在淮南就结甜橘子，种在淮北就结又小又苦的枳？

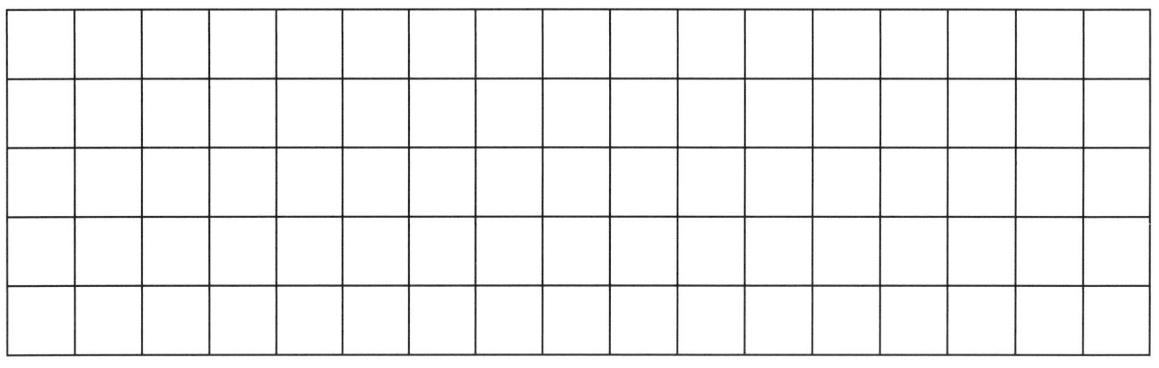

十三 分角色朗读课文两遍

## 第六课 张良拜师

### 一 写生词

| 韩 | | | | | | 礼 | 貌 | | | | |
| 灭 | | | | | | 恭 | 敬 | | | | |
| 懂 | | | | | | 耐 | 心 | | | | |
| 拾 | | | | | | 教 | 导 | | | | |
| 拜 | 师 | | | | | 约 | 会 | | | | |
| 功 | 臣 | | | | | 道 | 歉 | | | | |
| 刺 | 杀 | | | | | 推 | 翻 | | | | |
| 吃 | 惊 | | | | | | | | | | |

### 二 组词

拜 {_____  _____}　　约 {_____  _____}　　导 {_____  _____}

### 三 选字组词

（勺　约）会　　（韩　伟）国　　礼（貌　豹）

（勺　约）子　　（韩　伟）大　　花（貌　豹）

# 第六课 张良拜师

## 四 在方框中写字,再数笔画

| 貌 | 歉 | 恭 |

____画　　　____画　　　____画

## 五 选词填空

1. 张良原是_____人。(楚国　韩国　齐国)

2. 张良听了很吃惊,心想真不懂_____。(礼貌　花豹)

3. 张良刚想_____,老人瞪了他一眼。(道歉　道理)

4. 张良用心读书,_____得了用兵的道理。(重　懂)

## 六 根据课文判断对错

1. 张良是秦汉时期人,是秦朝的功臣。　　　___对___错

2. 张良原是韩国人,一心想刺杀秦始皇。　　___对___错

3. 张良恭恭敬敬地给老人穿上鞋。　　　　　___对___错

4. 张良碰上了有学问的老人。　　　　　　　___对___错

## 第六课 张良拜师

5. 老人给张良珍贵的宝刀。　　　　　　　　　___对___错

6. 张良善良又有耐心，所以老人教导他。　　　___对___错

## 七 造句

道歉_____

约会_____

## 八 根据课文写出老人（老师）考察张良的做法

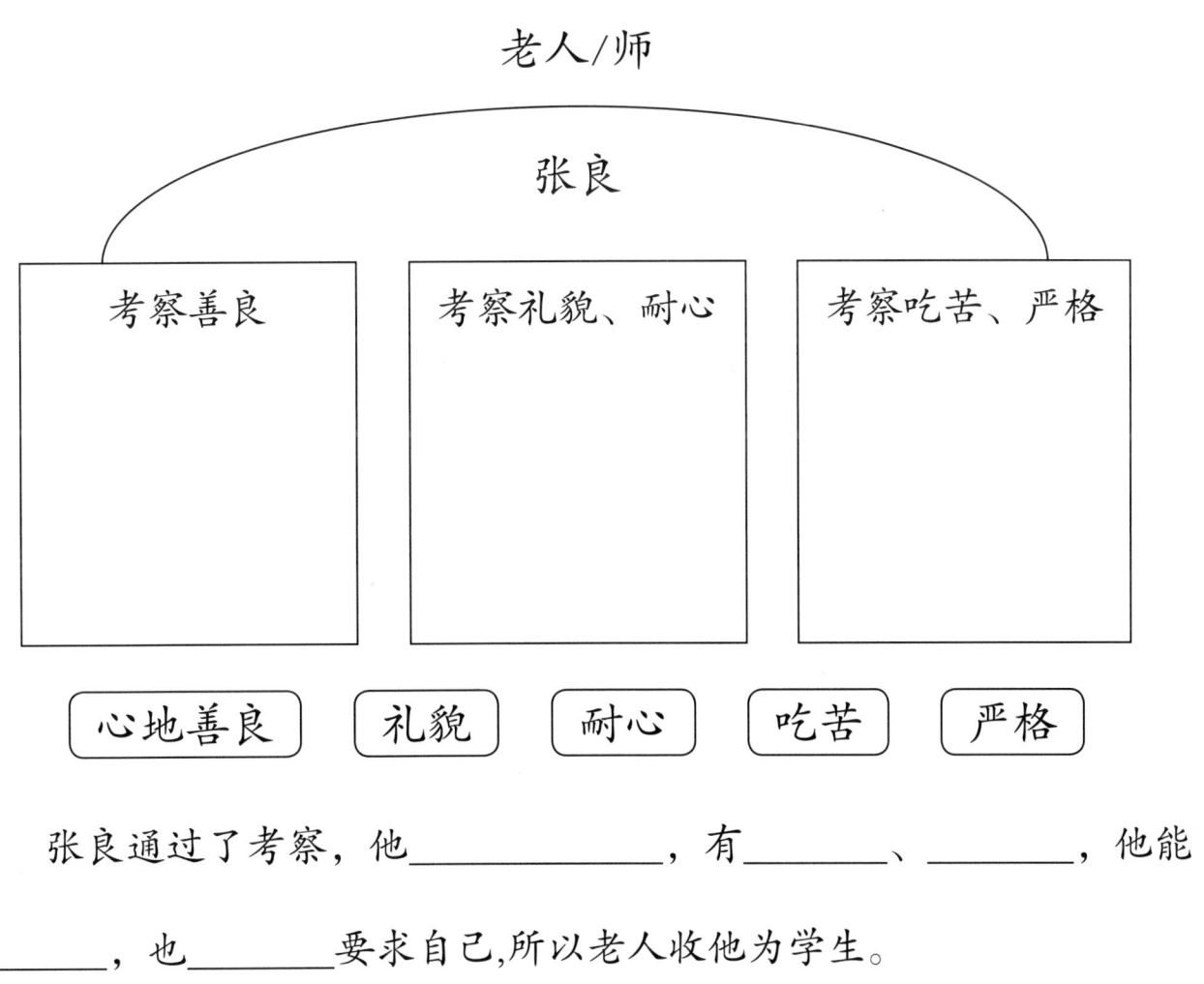

张良通过了考察，他_____，有_____、_____，他能_____，也_____要求自己，所以老人收他为学生。

# 第六课 张良拜师

## 九 选择填空

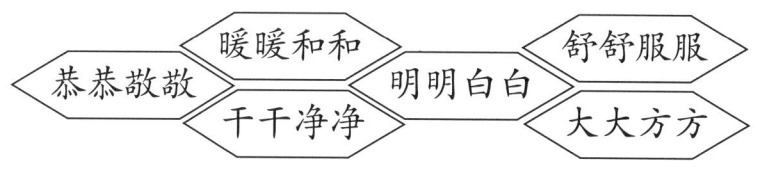
恭恭敬敬　暖暖和和　明明白白　舒舒服服　干干净净　大大方方

1. 冬天屋子要烧得＿＿＿＿＿的，奶奶才不会生病。

2. 学生们把教室打扫得＿＿＿＿＿的。

3. 李华有礼貌，对老人说话总是＿＿＿＿＿的。

4. 新来的同学＿＿＿＿＿地向大家介绍自己。

5. 姐姐学习好，因为她每道题都弄得＿＿＿＿＿的。

6. 星期日，我＿＿＿＿＿地睡了一大觉。

## 十 根据阅读《摸钟》判断对错

1. 县官抓来的几个人都说没偷东西。　　　　　＿＿对＿＿错

2. 县官让他们一个一个进屋摸钟。　　　　　　＿＿对＿＿错

3. 大钟一直没出声音。　　　　　　　　　　　＿＿对＿＿错

4. 县官看每个人的手。　　　　　　　　　　　＿＿对＿＿错

5. 只有两个人的手是干干净净的。　　　　　　＿＿对＿＿错

## 十一 朗读课文三遍

## 第八课 高山流水

一　写生词

| 若 |  |  |  |  |  |
|---|---|---|---|---|---|
| 飘 |  |  |  |  |  |
| 琴 | 艺 |  |  |  |  |
| 高 | 超 |  |  |  |  |
| 弹 | 琴 |  |  |  |  |
| 悠 | 扬 |  |  |  |  |
| 琴 | 弦 |  |  |  |  |
| 斧 | 头 |  |  |  |  |

| 巍 | 巍 |  |  |  |  |
|---|---|---|---|---|---|
| 如 | 此 |  |  |  |  |
| 知 | 音 |  |  |  |  |
| 欣 | 赏 |  |  |  |  |
| 美 | 妙 |  |  |  |  |
| 一 | 捆 | 柴 |  |  |  |
| 相 | 见 | 恨 | 晚 |  |  |
|   |   |   |   |   |   |

二　组词

超 { _____  
　　 _____

音 { _____  
　　 _____

琴 { _____  
　　 _____

此 { _____  
　　 _____

三　下列汉字是由哪些字组成的

巍 — 山 + 魏　　　　斧 — □ + □

妙 — □ + □　　　　弹 — □ + □

## 第八课 高山流水

**四 填写量词**

一（　　）柴　　　　一（　　）诗

一（　　）草　　　　一（　　）歌

**五 看看下图中的4个字是什么，请写出**

**六 选词填空**

1. 战国时期，楚国有一位＿＿＿＿伯牙。（琴师　老师）

2. 琴声＿＿＿＿，飘于山川天地之间。（悠扬　漂亮）

3. 一位樵夫在听琴，手里拿着一把＿＿＿＿。（斧头　父亲）

4. 钟子期脚边还有＿＿＿＿柴。（一块　一捆）

5. 伯牙看钟子期如此＿＿＿＿，非常感动。（知音　知识）

6. 伯牙抱着琴到钟子期坟前，为他＿＿＿＿。（弹琴　琴弦）

## 第八课 高山流水

### 七 根据课文判断对错

1. 中国古代有一首著名的乐曲叫《流水高山》。　　　___对___错

2. 战国时有一位琴师伯牙，他琴艺高超。　　　　　　___对___错

3. 伯牙弹琴时，琴弦突然断了。　　　　　　　　　　___对___错

4. 有一位官员叫钟子期在听琴。　　　　　　　　　　___对___错

5. 伯牙和钟子期成了知音。　　　　　　　　　　　　___对___错

6. 钟子期死后伯牙把琴摔了，不再弹琴了。　　　　　___对___错

### 八 造句

如此＿＿＿＿＿＿＿＿＿＿＿＿＿＿＿＿＿＿＿＿＿＿＿＿＿＿＿

### 九 将相关解释连线

| | |
|---|---|
| 月明风清 | 比喻"知音，知己" |
| 巍巍兮若泰山 | 认识得太晚了 |
| 相见恨晚 | 月光明朗小风清凉 |
| 人们用"高山流水" | 像泰山高大雄伟 |

## 第八课
### 高山流水

十 写出反义词

恨 ↔ ☐     忘 ↔ ☐

十一 读一读

知音——形容朋友之间的友情

十二 给敦煌壁画着色，注意古乐器

数数图中有几种乐器？_____种

请写出一种乐器的名字：_____

十三 朗读课文三遍

# 第十课
## 完璧归赵

☆ ------------ ☆ ------------ ☆

一 写生词

| 氏 |  |  |  |  |  |
|---|---|---|---|---|---|
| 献 |  |  |  |  |  |
| 捧 |  |  |  |  |  |
| 逼 |  |  |  |  |  |
| 封 |  |  |  |  |  |
| 上 | 当 |  |  |  |  |
| 进 | 攻 |  |  |  |  |
| 机 | 智 |  |  |  |  |

| 举 | 行 |  |  |  |  |
|---|---|---|---|---|---|
| 隆 | 重 |  |  |  |  |
| 典 | 礼 |  |  |  |  |
| 约 | 定 |  |  |  |  |
| 大 | 方 |  |  |  |  |
| 客 | 气 |  |  |  |  |
| 完 | 璧 | 归 | 赵 |  |  |

二 圈字组词，并将词组写出

| 典 | 进 | 隆 | 重 |
|---|---|---|---|
| 攻 | 礼 | 机 | 智 |
| 举 | 字 | 客 | 气 |
| 行 | 典 | 捧 | 着 |

1. _____  2. _____
3. _____  4. _____
5. _____  6. _____
7. _____  8. _____

三 下列汉字是由哪些部分组成的

攻 — ☐ + ☐　　　智 — ☐ + ☐

# 第十课 完璧归赵

## 四 选字组词

进（攻 功）　　字（点 典）　　机（智 知）

典（扎 礼）　　隆（撞 重）　　（必 心）须

## 五 按字帖写两组"完璧归赵"

☐☐☐☐　　　☐☐☐☐

## 六 写出反义词

大方　　　　机智

↕　　　　　↕

☐　　　　　☐

# 第十课 完璧归赵

## 七 选词填空

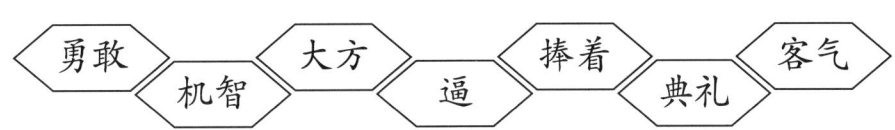

1. 蔺相如是一位_____、_____的人。

2. 秦王_____宝玉，连连说好。

3. 蔺相如说："您要是_____我，我的脑袋和宝玉就一块儿撞碎在柱子上！"

4. 蔺相如_____地对秦王说："宝玉送回去了。"

5. 蔺相如和秦王约定了_____的日期。

6. 秦王只得_____地送蔺相如回国。

## 八 根据课文判断对错

1. 战国时期，赵国很强，常常进攻别的国家。 ___对___错

2. 秦王愿意拿十座城来换和氏璧。 ___对___错

3. 赵国大臣蔺相如有办法。 ___对___错

4. 蔺相如拿着宝玉就要往柱子上撞。 ___对___错

5. 秦王怕宝玉碎了，连忙劝住蔺相如。 ___对___错

6. 蔺相如让人偷偷把宝玉送回秦国。 ___对___错

## 第十课 完璧归赵

**九 读下文写出蔺相如和秦王的表现**

- 秦王捧着宝玉，连连说好，就是不提交城换璧的事。

- 蔺相如说："大王，宝玉有点儿小毛病，让我指给您看。"

- 蔺相如接过宝玉说："我看您不想交出十五座城，所以把宝玉拿了回来。您要是逼我，我的脑袋和宝玉就撞碎在柱子上！"说着，举起宝玉就要往柱子上撞。

- 秦王还叫人拿出地图，把要给赵国的十五座城指给他看。

| 蔺相如机智勇敢 | 秦王并无真心 |
|---|---|
|  |  |

**十 造句**

约好_____

# 第十课 完璧归赵

十一 缩写课文《完璧归赵》，不少于8句，注意标点

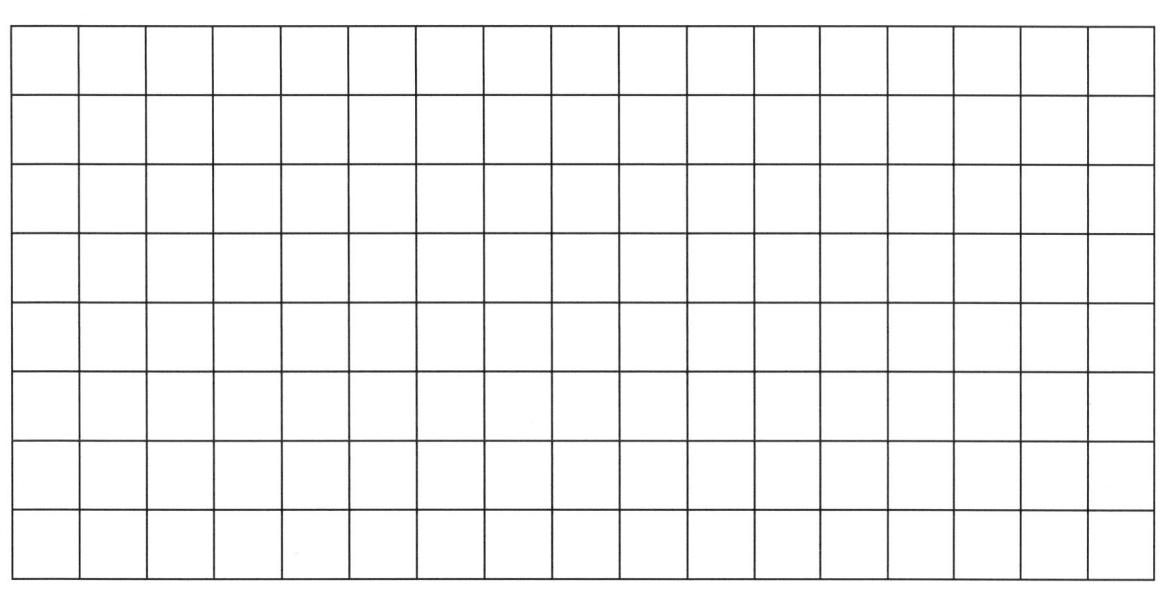

十二 根据阅读《荆轲刺秦王》选择填空

1. 荆轲刺秦王的故事发生在_____时期（战国　汉朝）

2. 荆轲拿地图给秦王看，图展开一把_____露出！（匕首　枪）

3. 荆轲抓住秦王的_____，拿起匕首向秦王刺去。（衣袖　背心）

4. 秦王挣断袖子，围着_____跑。（桌子　柱子）

5. 秦王拔出宝剑，砍伤了荆轲的_____。（腿　手）

6. 荆轲将匕首扔向秦王，匕首_____在柱子上。（落　扎）

7. 荆轲刺秦王_____了，可他是一位英雄。（成功　失败）

十三 分角色朗读课文

第二课   听写

| 1. | 2. | 3. | 4. |
| 5. | 6. | 7. | 8. |
| 9. | 10. | 11. | 12. |

第四课   听写

| 1. | 2. | 3. | 4. |
| 5. | 6. | 7. | 8. |
| 9. | 10. | 11. | 12. |

第六课   听写

| 1. | 2. | 3. | 4. |
| 5. | 6. | 7. | 8. |
| 9. | 10. | 11. | 12. |

第八课   听写

| 1. | 2. | 3. | 4. |
| 5. | 6. | 7. | 8. |
| 9. | 10. | 11. | 12. |

第十课　听写

| 1. | 2. | 3. | 4. |
| 5. | 6. | 7. | 8. |
| 9. | 10. | 11. | 12. |

| 1. | 2. | 3. | 4. |
| 5. | 6. | 7. | 8. |
| 9. | 10. | 11. | 12. |

| 1. | 2. | 3. | 4. |
| 5. | 6. | 7. | 8. |
| 9. | 10. | 11. | 12. |

| 1. | 2. | 3. | 4. |
| 5. | 6. | 7. | 8. |
| 9. | 10. | 11. | 12. |